Playing God

Playing God

Talking About Ethics in Medicine and Technology

Edited by Tony Watkins

Cover design by fourninezero design.
Typeset by GCS, Leighton Buzzard, Beds,
in 11 on 13 Palatino
Print management by Adare Carwin
Printed in the UK by J.H. Haynes & Co., Sparkford

Contents

Introduction to the *Talking About* Series

Have you ever had one of those conversations when you know you ought to be able to bring in a Christian perspective? The problem is how to do it. As the conversation goes on you become more and more anxious. You know you have a good opportunity to say something; you know you *should* say something – but you just can't think what. Probably all of us have been there at some time or other. Many of us would like a little help on thinking through some issues beforehand.

It seems to me that there are three areas of conversation which frequently cry out for a Christian angle to be included: personal issues in the lives of friends, family or work colleagues; big issues in society generally; and things in the media. They often overlap, of course. So when Nick Pollard was asked to contribute a regular column for *Idea*, the Evangelical Alliance's magazine for members,[1] it seemed a great opportunity to focus on some of the overlapping issues which people are talking about. The articles aim to help readers understand some of what is being said about these issues in today's world, and particularly to explore some of the underlying ideas. The primary aim, of course, is to help equip people for having more and more productive conversations with friends, colleagues and family. It soon became apparent that this is just the kind of help that many Christians feel they need.

So, this series of short books came to be. Each of the books takes the basic ingredients of what Nick has written in one of his articles and develops them into something more substantial, but still light and easily digested. Nick significantly develops his 800-word *Idea* article into the opening chapter of each book. Then come some extra ingredients: a biblical perspective on the issue; articles on key aspects of the central theme; study guides on relevant films, books or television programmes; and an introduction to one or more key thinkers whose work still influences our culture. Some of these chapters have been developed from material published on Damaris' CultureWatch website (www. culturewatch.org), others have been commissioned especially for this book. Finally, sprinkled throughout the mix are some great quotes which help to spice up your conversations about the issues we're examining (many of these quotes have come from another great Damaris resource, www.ToolsForTalks.com – a collection of tools for speakers whether they are teaching the Bible to Christians or engaged in evangelism).[2]

This is not the kind of book to sit down and read straight through. Instead it has been designed for dipping into. Each of the chapters stands independently of the others, though of course they're all linked by the common theme. One of the consequences of this is that you will, at times, find a little overlap between chapters. We've minimised this as much as we can without taking away anything essential from one or more of the chapters. The study guides are suitable for individual reflection or for use in home groups. If you do use them in a group setting, don't slavishly work through all the questions – we've given you more than enough so that you can select some that you feel are particularly helpful to your group. Finally, the last chapter, introducing an influential thinker, is inevitably harder going than earlier chapters – which is why it is at the end of the book. It is worth taking time to try to understand the line of argument and why it is significant, but the chapter is not essential for getting to grips with the central issue around which the book revolves.

We hope you will find this interesting, entertaining and stimulating. But our prayer is that this will enable you to be more effective in talking about the good news of Jesus Christ within today's world, whether – as Nick frequently says – you are talking from a pulpit or over the garden fence.

Tony Watkins

Notes

[1] For more information, contact Evangelical Alliance at 186 Kennington Park Road, London, SE11 4BT or visit their website: www.eauk.org
[2] All addresses of websites listed in this book were accessed at the end of January 2006. However, please bear in mind that some of these sites may move their material to new locations in the future.

Acknowledgements

I am extremely grateful to all the writers who have contributed to this book, and to the series as a whole. It is a joy to work with people who are so committed to thoroughly analysing facets of our culture in order to help Christians in their discipleship and evangelism, and to help those who are not yet Christians begin to see the extraordinary relevance of the Christian faith.

Particular thanks go to Nick Pollard whose insightful writing is the foundation for the books, and who provides many helpful suggestions on material for inclusion. We are grateful to Eleanor Margesson for her article on *Oryx and Crake* on CultureWatch, some of which was incorporated into Caroline Puntis's chapter. Thanks also to Steve Couch, Managing Editor of Damaris Books, for his constant support during the many stages of pulling the books together, and to the team at Authentic Media who handle the production of the books and with whom we enjoy a strong partnership.

Introduction

'Let our baby live,' said the headline. As soon as I picked up the newspaper, this sparked a conversation with other people in the checkout queue. And since then, this particular story has caused much more discussion across the country and, indeed, across the world.

The headline was placed above a photo of a little baby called Charlotte Wyatt. At the time she was just eleven months old and she was seriously ill with heart and lung problems.[1] In fact, the doctors were describing her life as 'dominated by pain and suffering'. This was because when she was born, she was three months premature and was only five inches long.

And so the question arose, if she should stop breathing, should she be resuscitated or should she be left to die? This was a difficult question, and one which has caused a great deal of debate at all levels. The case was eventually taken to the High Court, and there, on 7 October 2004, the judge ruled that she should be given proper medical care, but not intubation and ventilation. That is, if she stopped breathing she would not be artificially resuscitated. Instead, she would be cared for as she died. In January, March and April 2005, the parents sought, unsuccessfully, to have this verdict overruled. And then, in October 2005, the judge altered his ruling, saying that the doctors do not have to leave her to die, but that they will not be committing a crime if they decide to do that. Throughout this period, most people in Britain heard about baby Charlotte and would readily talk about the rights and wrongs of the judge's decision.

Meanwhile, in America, another case was causing an equal amount of discussion. This concerned an adult by the name of Terri Schiavo. She was being kept alive by equipment that was artificially providing her with food and water. But she was, apparently, seriously brain damaged, and in what many doctors call a Persistent Vegitative State. So, the question was whether she should be continually fed and watered in this way, or whether she should be left to die.

Again, this became the subject of many legal battles involving everyone from junior lawyers to the President of the United States. Eventually, on 18 March 2005, the feeding tubes were finally removed and she was left to die. As in Britain with baby Charlotte, so with this case in the USA, most people would readily talk about the rights and wrongs of the judge's decisions.

One of the significant features of both of these cases is the fact that they were new ethical dilemmas, caused by new developments in medical technology. It is not very long ago that no one would have been able to keep Terri alive. In the same way, it is not long ago that a baby like Charlotte would certainly have died at birth. But now things have changed. Our rapidly developing technology is creating many more ethical dilemmas than people faced even just a few years ago. And these, in turn, provoke a lot of discussion about the underlying spiritual and moral questions of life.

So, how do we face them? Logical rational science has created these dilemmas, so should we use logic and reason to consider and respond to them? And, if so, what does it really mean to be logical and rational about such issues? Indeed, does Christian faith lead us to take a broader view of logic and reason as we seek to consider the big questions of life? In particular, what is the place of intuition and revelation? However we handle such questions – and different Christians will have different approaches to them – there is no doubt that the recent developments in medical science have put big questions on many people's lips.

This presents a great challenge as well as a great opportunity for Christians. The challenge is being able to talk clearly and helpfully with people who are seeking answers to these questions. The opportunity is that this leads many to a consideration of the life and teaching of Jesus. So, if we are going to be able to help people at this crucial time, we must give adequate thought to the issues ourselves. That is what this book is designed to help you to do.

Nick Pollard

Note

[1] See 'Q&A: The Charlotte Wyatt Case' on BBC News for more background to this case – news.bbc.co.uk/2/hi/health/3724194.stm

I'd much rather be happy than right any day.

Slartibartfast in the film *The Hitchhiker's Guide to the Galaxy*

1. Rethinking Life and Death

Nick Pollard

President George Bush cut short his Easter holiday because he felt so strongly about the issue and he wanted to sign an unprecedented Emergency Bill. Almost every other American had an opinion on the matter. The subject dominated the newspapers, the radio and the television. It was discussed in lecture halls, churches and bars. And what were they all talking about? It was the fact that the courts had ruled that food and water should be withdrawn from a desperately ill young woman so that she would die.

Terri Schiavo was 26 when she fell into what doctors call a Persistent Vegitative State (PVS). In this case it was apparently as the result of brain damage due to her heart stopping temporarily. For the next fifteen years she was unable to speak, move or feed herself. There was no doubt that she was now living in a very sick body. But there was a lot of dispute about whether she was at peace or in torment, and whether it was her wish to be kept alive by the food and water tubes connected to her body, or whether she would rather have them removed so that she could die.

The two different views were championed by her parents – who wanted to keep her alive – and her husband – who wanted her to die. During the spring of 2005, much of the world joined in the debate. Eventually, the legal process ruled in favour of the husband and, on 18 March 2005, the feeding tubes were finally removed. Over the next thirteen days the world watched as she died. No one viewed Terri as closely as her parents who sat by her bedside and later said:

> Watching someone being starved and dehydrated to death, let alone your own daughter, is something so cruel that it can never be forgotten.... Witnessing her life ebbing away as she desperately struggled for a breath of air is beyond the realm of human comprehension.[1]

As desperate as one feels for Terri's parents, and for Terri herself, we must recognise that there is another group of people who were also there and will also have felt a huge amount of anguish and pain: the doctors and nurses. They trained for years to help and heal sick people; their desire is always to do the best for their patients. But now they find themselves being asked to 'play God'. It is the doctors and nurses who removed Terri's tubes. And, as we saw in the introduction, it is the doctors and nurses who will not resuscitate baby Charlotte when she stops breathing.

A Fork in the Road

The incidence of such situations is increasing relentlessly, mainly because of continual advances in medical science. Not many years ago, medics would have been unable to keep Terri or Charlotte alive. But now things have changed – and they keep on changing. What is more, these changes are not restricted only to improvements in the delivery of traditional medical techniques. They also seem to offer entirely new ways of understanding and dealing with human beings. Indeed, they seem to promise a brave new world free from sickness, pain and even death. This is evidently the ultimate goal of research into such areas as cloning, genetic modification, stem cell research, nano-technology, and genetic selection.

There are those who argue that we should embrace such developments with open arms and move as fast as we can into this wonderful new world. Gregory Stock, Director of the Program on Medicine, Technology, and Society at UCLA's School of Public Health, is one of those. His book *Redesigning Humans*[2] argues that we should use technology to develop the human race. He believes that the continued progress of medical technology is inevitable, and the sooner we get on with using it, the better it will be for all of us.

On the other hand there are others, such as Francis Fukuyama from John Hopkins University, who urge much more caution. His book *Our Posthuman Future: Consequences of the Biotechnology Revolution*[3] argues that human genetic engineering is not inevitable and that we should take steps to prevent the possible 'abolition of man'.

Creating Life and Death

While this debate rages at an academic level, it also does so at a much more popular level. As with all great questions in life, the creative writers and producers of novels, films, music and television programmes contribute to the discussion. They have a lot of influence on many people's thinking about the issues. Indeed, most people are influenced more directly by the ideas expressed in popular media than they are by the arguments taking place in academia (although, of course, that academic work trickles down through its influence on writers and producers). Therefore, as we seek to consider how as Christians we are going to engage meaningfully with others about these questions, we must consider the ideas being explored in popular culture. Here are a few examples:

The film *Godsend*[4] tells the story of Paul and Jessie Duncan (Greg Kinnear and Rebecca Romijn-Stamos) who are the devoted parents of Adam (Cameron Bright). When he is eight years old, Adam is killed in a car accident. This devastates his parents, not least because Jessie is unable to have any more children. However, help is offered by Dr Richard Wells (Robert De Niro), a prominent fertility expert now working secretly on cloning technology. Taking material from Adam's body, he makes an exact biological replica. For the first eight years of his life, this second Adam grows up without any problems. However, when he passes the age at which the first Adam died, he starts to change. He has nightmares – and his dreams seem to belong to another boy.

Thus the film does not only explore the ethical questions raised by the development of cloning technology (and whether this could or should be applied to humans), it also digs much deeper into the spiritual questions of human existence, and what it means to be a human person.

Such questions are considered from a different angle by Jodi Picoult in her book *My Sister's Keeper*.[5] This tells the story of sisters Anna and Kate. Kate is sixteen and had suffered from leukaemia for most of her life. Anna is thirteen and is the means by which her parents seek to provide the medical solution to Kate's disease – she was conceived through IVF so that she would be able to serve her sister as a donor. But now Anna is not so happy with her role. She wants to be free from the control of her parents and the needs of her sister. Can she do this? Should she do this? Who has the right to decide what happens to anyone's body? These are just some of the questions raised by this book.

Spare Parts

Then, in 2005, came a film that took the issues raised by *Godsend* and *My Sister's Keeper* onto a whole new level. *The Island*[6] tells the story of a medical establishment that uses cloning to create bodies as replacement parts for those who might need them. Like *Godsend*, the film is about cloning enabling people to avoid the consequences of accidents and disease. But unlike in *Godsend*, the cloning takes place before someone dies so that replacement parts are prepared in advance, ready for when they are needed. Like *My Sister's Keeper*, the technology in *The Island* is used to provide transplant resources in order to save the life of someone who is sick. But unlike in *My Sister's Keeper*, removing those resources means that the clone must be killed in order for the required organs to be 'harvested'.

The whole drama of *The Island* centres around the expectation that we, the viewers, will identify with the clones that are soon to be killed rather than with the original people whose lives are to be saved. Thus we follow the story of Lincoln Six Echo (Ewan McGregor) and Jordan Two Delta (Scarlett Johansson) as they begin to realise that something is wrong, and as they escape from the laboratory, track down the people from whom they were cloned, and eventually confront the scientist behind the technology, Doctor Merrick (Sean Bean).

It is possible to feel some sympathy for Doctor Merrick. It seems that he began as a compassionate doctor with good motives who wanted to do the best for his patients. He thought that he would achieve this by using the most advanced technology, and at one point in the film he describes how he had reluctantly found himself moving step-by-step to what he was doing now. Perhaps this glimpse of the situation from the doctor's perspective makes us think more deeply about the seductive power of continually advancing medical technology – and the need to think carefully about what we are doing.

Do No Harm

We may think that an equivalent of Dr Merrick's slide into a barbaric treatment of human life would never happen in the real world. Surely we have checks and balances that will prevent such abuses. But can we actually be so sure? Is it possible to have a set of logical and reasonable rules that will protect us from potential harm? That was an idea that was considered in another film, *I Robot*.[7] Like many other recent films, it explores the possible impact of advancing technology on life as we know it, but this time it focuses on robotics and artificial intelligence.

I, Robot is set in a future where robots are a part of everyone's life. They do the work that no one else wants to do – they shop, they clean, they serve the food and drink, and then clean up the rubbish afterwards.

This sounds wonderful, and wonderfully safe because of the so-called First Law of Robotics that: 'A robot may not harm a human nor, through inactivity, allow a human to come to harm.' But it is that law which the film seeks to explore. The question *I, Robot* poses is, will this entirely logical and reasonable law protect us from the adverse impact of developing technology? It is interesting that this fictional law[8] parallels an actual fundamental principle in real life medical ethics. This is the rule that dates back to Hippocrates, is accepted by every doctor, and is usually expressed as *primum non nocere* or 'first do no harm'. This may seem a perfectly good safeguard for today's doctors and tomorrow's robots. And such reasonable logic appeals to those who are using logic and reason to advance medical technology. But, *I, Robot* seeks to highlight some limitations of apparently reasonable logic.

In the film, a supercomputer accepts the first law of robotics, as it is programmed to do, and seeks to do everything it can to protect humans. But then it looks at the fact that, left to themselves, humans have a tendency to be violent towards one another. Through the choices they make, these humans are causing *each other* harm. So, the supercomputer concludes that the best way to protect humans is to stop them from hurting each other by taking away their freedom. Indeed, it has a sense of urgency since it knows that it must not allow humans to come to harm by its inactivity: it has to do something quickly. Therefore, this computer establishes control over a new series of robots and seeks to use them to take over the world so that they can make it a safer place for humans. Claiming to have flawless logic, the computer also concludes that it is acceptable to kill certain humans during the take-over since this will save more lives in the future.

Meanwhile, *The Stepford Wives*[9] explores the same question from a different angle. The geeky men of Stepford have created perfect robotic replacements for their wives and now enjoy an idyllic life where their 'wives' serve them in every possible way. When a new man arrives in Stepford, the other men try to persuade him of the logical value of replacing his troubled and troublesome wife. He can see how attractive this solution is. Indeed, the logic for replacing his wife with a perfect robot is very compelling. But he refuses to follow this logic and he eventually exposes the deception. Why does he do this? The film makes it clear: it is because he loves her, with all her faults and failings. It is such a love that also provides the resolution to the *I, Robot* story. In the final scene we watch the hero argue for the importance of compassion over and above logical reasoning.

Dare to be Wise

The use of logical reasoning in ethics has a long philosophical history. It became particularly influential through the period of the seventeenth and eighteenth century (which is known as the Age of Reason or the Enlightenment). This was a time when many philosophers encouraged people to think for themselves rather than just blindly following church dogma. For example, Immanuel Kant, one of the key thinkers of the period, had a catch-phrase which he thought summed up what was needed. *'Sapere aude,'* he said. This means literally 'dare to be wise' and was taken to mean 'dare to think it out for yourself'. And so it was that the culture that was built upon these enlightenment principles (a culture that is sometimes referred to as Modernism) came to prize logic and reason.

In the twentieth century, there has been a gradual move from Modernism to Postmodernism for many people, which has led some of them away from a confidence in logic and reason. However, many more continue to recognise the value of logic. This is especially the case for those working in technology because it is logic and reason that enables them to advance their technology. And so it is logic and reason that they seek to apply when considering the ethical issues raised by the advance of that technology.

Perhaps the clearest example of this is Peter Singer. Whilst he is a philosopher rather than a technologist, his particular interest is in working through the ethical implications of advances in biotechnology. He is the founding co-editor of the journal *Bioethics* and is a professor at the Princeton University Center for Human Values. Singer has written at length on what he sees as the logical and reasonable decisions we should make in response to the ethical dilemmas of today – and he is not afraid to set aside traditional beliefs and values in order to seek new ways of responding to new challenges. For example, his book *Rethinking Life and Death*[10] is subtitled 'the collapse of our traditional ethics'. In it he argues that our traditional ways of thinking about life and death cannot cope with the strain of extremely complex and painful medical dilemmas which have arisen in recent years as medical technology has vastly enhanced the ability of doctors to save and prolong life.

The Unimportance of Being Human

Singer claims that it is no longer possible to take the sanctity of life as the cornerstone of our ethical outlook. We must sweep away the old ethic and construct something new in its place. Building something new requires a foundation – a set of principles from which to begin. And so, one of the major principles Singer adopts is the modern secular humanist distinction between a 'human being' and a 'human person'. Specifically, Singer argues that a human being is a biological member of the species *Homo Sapiens*, but a human person is someone who is far more than that. A person, according to Singer, is conscious, aware of itself as the same being in different times and places, and capable of anticipating the future as well as of having wants and desires for that future.

This distinction is very important for Singer because he then seeks to argue logically that the fact that someone is a human being does not give them the same right to life as a human person. So, he argues that those who are in a Persistent Vegitative State and those with severe intellectual disabilities may be human beings but they are not human persons. Therefore, he says, killing them would not always be wrong – and, indeed, in many cases would be the very best thing to do.

However, he does not stop there. He then applies his relentless logic to the case of newborn babies. He points out that all newborn babies are actually in that same category. He says that in the first few weeks of life these newborn babies have no sense of their existence over time – they are not capable of anticipating the future nor of having wants and desires for that future. Therefore, he argues that 'killing a newborn baby is never equivalent to killing a person.' And, in case of any doubt, he does mean actively killing the baby, not just letting them die. He adds, 'if a decision is taken, by the parents and doctors, that it is better that a baby should die, I believe it should be possible to carry out that decision . . . by taking active steps to end the baby's life swiftly and humanely.'[11]

Singing Another Tune

So how do we respond to such a position? Here are three possible ways:

First, one might agree with him that this is entirely logical and reasonable. Thus, one might accept his belief and look for ways of applying it in every possible situation – in every case like baby Charlotte and Terri Schiavo.

Secondly, one might accept that this is an entirely logical position, but then argue that this shows the danger of a narrow view of reason. This was an approach expressed in the famous words of Blaise Pascal who said, 'The heart has its reasons that reason knows not of.' For Pascal, and others who hold this view, logic is important but requires a broader view of reason which recognises the value of intuition and even the possibility of revelation. If people are prepared to consider those possibilities, perhaps we will want to talk with them about the possibility that there might be a God who could reveal truth to us – maybe directly through scripture or indirectly through the conscience he has given us.

Thirdly, one might question the soundness of his argument. An argument is simply a process that links together two premises (two claims about reality) in order to formulate a conclusion. Thus an argument can be expressed as:

Premise

Premise

Conclusion

Philosophers call this a *syllogism*. The classic example
of this was given by the ancient Greek philosopher
Aristotle (which is why it is often referred to as
'Aristotelian Syllogistic Logic') who gave this example:

Premise: Socrates is a man

Premise: All men will die

Conclusion: Therefore Socrates will die

That is a sound argument. However, there are three
ways in which an argument may be unsound. First,
it may use invalid logic. That is, the conclusion may
not follow logically from the two premises. Second,
the terms may be ambiguous. That is, words may be
used to mean different things at different times. Third,
the premises may be false. That is, one or both of the
two premises may actually be untrue claims about the
world.

So, looking at the argument that Singer uses, we
might ask whether it is sound or whether it falls into
the trap of using invalid logic, ambiguous terms or
false premises. To consider this we must first express
his argument as a syllogism, perhaps as follows:

Premise: Humans do not have an automatic right to life if
they have no sense of their existence over time

Premise: Newborn babies have no sense of their existence
over time

Conclusion: Therefore newborn babies do not have an
automatic right to life

We might then conclude that this argument is logically
valid, and does not use ambiguous terms. But are the
premises true? We might accept the second premise

(although we might question how we could ever know). But is the first premise a true claim about the world? Or is it just an assertion that he makes? Where does he get this from? Why should anyone accept this assertion rather than an alternative such as, 'Humans have value, significance and rights because they are created by God in his image'?

Thus, we are then back in the same kind of territory where we were in the second response to Singer – considering the possibility that there might be a God who reveals his truth to us. And that is a very good place to be when we are talking with people about these questions. We want to help people to understand the issues; we want to respond to the specific views that are expressed in our culture. But we particularly want people to listen to the Bible which says, 'When we tell you this, we do not use words of human wisdom. We speak words given to us by the Spirit, using the Spirit's words to explain spiritual truths' (1 Cor. 2:13).

Notes

[1] See www.terrisfight.org

[2] Gregory Stock, *Redesigning Humans* (Profile Books, 2002)

[3] Francis Fukuyama, *Our Posthuman Future: Consequences of the Biotechnology Revolution* (Profile Books, 2002). For an article critiquing Stock's and Fukuyama's books, see Peter S. Williams, 'Mere Humanity', *CultureWatch* – www.damaris.org/content/content.php?type=5&id=92

[4] Directed by Nick Hamm (Lion Gate Films, 2004). For a study guide on *Godsend*, see Louise Crook, 'Godsend', *CultureWatch* – www.damaris.org/content/content.php?type=1&id=224

[5] Jodi Picoult, *My Sister's Keeper* (Atria Books, 2004). For a study guide on this book, see chapter seven.

[6] Directed by Michael Bay (DreamWorks, 2005). For a study guide on *The Island*, see chapter eight.

[7] Directed by Alex Proyas (Twentieth Century Fox, 2004). For more on *I, Robot*, see chapter five. For a study guide, see Tony Watkins, 'I, Robot', *CultureWatch* – www.damaris.org/content/content.php?type=1&id=202

[8] For more on the Three Laws of Robotics, see chapter five.

[9] Directed by Frank Oz (Paramount, 2004). See also Louise Crook, 'Flawed Perfection', *CultureWatch* – www.damaris.org/content/content.php?type=5&id=392

[10] Peter Singer, *Rethinking Life and Death* (Oxford University Press, 1995)

[11] Peter Singer, FAQ, III. The Sanctity of Human Life – www.princeton.edu/~psinger/faq.html

Sometimes we forget the rules are there for a reason.

JD in *Scrubs*

2. I Give You Dominion: A Biblical Perspective on Ethics in Medicine and Technology

Dr Trevor Stammers

> Can theology aim at understanding technology? Can we put the words *God* and *technology* together in any kind of meaningful sentence? Can theology guess what God is doing in today's technology? Or by our silence do we leave it utterly godless? Can we have a theology of technology that comprehends, gives meaning to, dares to influence the direction and set limits to this explosion of new powers?
>
> Ronald Cole-Turner[1]

These are vital questions with which twenty-first century Christians must engage. Theology is primarily concerned with God and the relation of ourselves and the universe to him. It focuses on God's purposes for humanity and the way we should live in the light of them. Science also aims to achieve ordered knowledge about ourselves and the universe. However, it focuses on structures, properties and functions. Science may be considered to be about *describing* reality, whereas technology, which may be defined as 'the systematic modification of the environment for human ends',[2] is about *transforming* reality. In practice, however, science and technology are deeply interwoven. Both increasingly influence all our lives, yet neither can give an adequate answer to the question, 'Why am I?'

The Two Books

Science and theology are also closely linked. 'Science affects the way theology is expressed, just as theology provides the beliefs about the world underlying science.'[3] The disproportionate publicity afforded to the views of scientists who are atheists, such as Richard Dawkins, should not cloud the fact that many of the leading figures in the development of science in the western world in the sixteenth to nineteenth centuries, such as Kepler, Boyle, Harvey, Newton, Joule, Faraday, Kelvin, Maxwell and Mendel were all theists. James Clerk Maxwell, the father of electromagnetic theory of light, saw to it that over the door of the Cavendish laboratory in Cambridge (scene of many early breakthroughs in nuclear physics) were inscribed the words of Psalm 111:2, which in a modern translation reads:

> How amazing are the deeds of the Lord!
> All who delight in him should ponder them.[4]

It is no coincidence that these eminent scientists were all believers in God. Francis Bacon (1561–1626) believed that God had spoken through two great Books: the Book of Nature and the Book of Scripture. Both the world ('the Book of God's works') and the Bible ('the Book of God's words') revealed God in different, but not contradictory, ways. As Psalm 19 expresses it:

> The heavens tell of the glory of God.
> The skies display his marvellous craftsmanship. (v. 1)

And

> The law of the Lord is perfect reviving the soul.
> The decrees of the Lord are trustworthy, making wise the
> simple. (v. 7)

As Ian Barbour suggests in his seminal work, *Issues in Science and Religion:* 'The choice is not between "faith" and "no-faith" but only faith in what? For man's ultimate loyalties and objects of devotion are not established by reason alone.'[5] Reijer Hooykaas, former Professor of the History of Science at the University of Utrecht, agrees with Barbour, insisting that, 'Scientific method rests on the preconceptions the scientist has about nature, and those preconceptions depend on, amongst other things, his belief about God.'[6] This chapter examines what the Bible teaches about God in relation to the development of scientific technology, and applies these biblical perspectives to some contemporary issues in biomedicine.

What Makes us Human?

The creation narratives of Genesis 1 and 2 are extraordinarily relevant to the heart of the biotechnology debate, as they set out the unique significance of humanity as being marked by the *imago Dei* – the image of God (Gen. 1:26–27) – and as having received God's command to rule over the rest of the created universe (Gen. 1:26,28–31). Professor Nigel Cameron believes that the major bioethical dilemmas of the twenty-first century have their root in this 'fateful ... meeting point of the dominion mandate and the *imago Dei*'.[7] For the first time in history, humanity created in God's image is on the verge of being able to create and modify our own species in ways that were in the realm of science fiction only a few decades ago.

Two crucial issues arise from the creation account: What makes us human? And what does the command to 'rule over the earth' entail?

'Whose likeness and inscription is this?' (Mt. 22:20, ESV) asks Jesus, showing a Roman denarius with Caesar's image on it. Just as that image was the physical symbol of the Emperor's authority and sovereignty over the Roman world, so those made in God's image are to represent God on planet Earth. This image of God is species-specific. *All* humans and *only* humans bear the Creator's image in this special sense. Vinoth Ramachandra notes this uniqueness of the *imago Dei*:

> Human beings alone are addressed by God. To the Creator, we exist not only as his objects, but his subjects. Human uniqueness consists not in the fact that we talk with each other, rather that God talks to us and invites us to reply. In other words *we are invited to become a part of the conversation that is the divine life.*[8]

Some contemporary bioethicists such as Peter Singer, Jonathan Glover and Helga Kuhse[9] see nothing intrinsically wrong in the killing of babies and young children because at such a young age, infants have no concept of death. Such philosophers consider that the handicapped, the demented and the brain-damaged are 'lives not worth living', and hence it is not only practical, but compassionate to humanely kill them. Clearly for these leading philosophers, 'being human' is defined in terms of ability and possession of particular functions. In contrast, the Bible defines our humanity by what we are, not by what we can or cannot do; not in terms of faculties we may or may not possess, but by the One who possesses us.

After the Fall – humanity falling for the serpent's lie that, in disobeying God's command they would themselves become 'like God' (Gen. 3:4) – Adam and Eve no longer see each other as unique creations of God to be respected and cherished (Gen. 2:23–25). Instead, they become pawns in a game of self-assertion and passing blame (Gen. 3:12–13). It is not at all surprising that, having lost respect for the image of God, the first murder soon follows. When there is doubt about the answer to the question, 'Am I my brother's keeper?' (Gen. 4:3–10, NIV), it is so much easier to kill.

As we shall see in the next section, the Bible is not anti-technology, but when today's biotechnology promises to enhance our humanity and make us as gods, we should recognise the echoes of Genesis (and Nietzsche[10]) and take heed.

Kevin Warwick, Professor of Cybernetics at Reading, who became the world's first 'cyborg' in 2001 when he had a chip implanted in his arm, declares, 'I was born human. But that was an accident of fate – a condition merely of time and place. I believe it's something we have the power to change.'[11] But if we change from being human into being something else, will what we become make a better world? Without a transformation of the heart (Ezek. 11:19), cybernetic transhumanism[12] is unlikely to improve our capacity to care, to love and to show compassion. As with ancient Israel, God may allow the transhumanist movement to have its way, but a 'plague' or 'leanness of soul' may well be the price paid for it (Ps. 106:15).

Stewards and Shapers

The divine command to rule or 'have dominion over' the earth (Gen. 1:26) is not a mandate to do with the planet just as we please. On the contrary, the Bible teaches that the entire universe, including ourselves, was created for God and for his pleasure (Rev. 4:11). The Hebrew words for 'rule' *(radah)* and 'subdue' *(kabash)*, though often having an oppressive context in a fallen world, could not have done so in a perfect creation which God declared wholly good (Gen. 1:4,10,12,18,21,25,31). In context, 'subdue' and 'rule over' do not justify exploitation and pollution of the earth but, in harmony with God's command to Adam to 'take care of it' (Gen. 2:15), are 'rather interpreted to mean: investigate and understand, control and direct and care for and develop. Technology certainly seems to facilitate such endeavours.'[13]

There are two main theological models within which an understanding of the cultivation of and care for the earth has been framed.

The model of *stewardship* emphasises conservation and care. As John Calvin expressed it:

> Let everyone regard himself as the steward of God in all things which he possesses. Then he will neither conduct himself dissolutely, not corrupt by abuse those things which God requires to be preserved.[14]

It focuses on the ownership of the earth by God and sees creation as a gift from God to be administered faithfully on his behalf. Far from conceiving 'dominion' as carte-blanche to plunder the earth's riches, 'the Judeo-Christian peoples were probably the first to develop on a large scale a pervasive concern for land management and an ethic of nature.'[15]

On the other hand, the *co-creator* model focuses on our human creativity and ability to transform our environment. Theologian Karl Rahner has emphasised the importance of humanity as *self-creator*, especially in regard to the use of biotechnology.[16] However, Rahner does not deny our human limitations, and emphasises that 'self-creator' is not to be 'understood in terms of one who makes something out of nothing.'[17]

Perhaps Philip Hefner's term of *created co-creators*,[18] though more wordy, is less ambiguous. For him, people are seen as 'one of the many agents of change that God allows to participate in his creative work. Human beings' creativity can be channelled so they co-create with God.'[19] Here again, however, within the very phrase 'created co-creator' we are twice reminded that ultimately we are resourced by the Creator himself, and rooted in the same creation that, by his gift, we are able to manipulate.

Babel's Shadow

Certainly Christians have good cause to celebrate and marvel in the wonders of the universe. 'Till you can sing and rejoice and delight in God, as misers do in gold and kings in sceptres, you never enjoy the World',[20] enthused Thomas Traherne in the sixteenth century. How much more should we delight in and worship the Creator of the human genome, black holes and quantum physics! The question of worship, however, leads us to the first of two limits which we allow technology to cross at our peril.

First, technology itself should never become the object of our worship. Many modern writers have warned of this danger in the graphic neologisms of 'genohype' and 'technolatry', but the roots of these new terms are as ancient as Babel itself. The people of Shinar aimed to use their technology to make a name for themselves by building the tallest tower on earth (Gen. 11:4). God does not have a problem with skyscrapers, but when he sees their godless motivation and the dangers of a future where 'nothing they plan to do will be impossible' (Gen.11:6, NIV), he frustrates the whole project and the tower is never completed.

We who live in Babel's shadow need to beware of technology either becoming our god or the means whereby we become gods. Richard Jastrow's longing for invincibility and immortality clearly inspires him, but, from a scriptural standpoint, such a vision is deeply troubling:

> Housed in indestructible lattices of silicon, and no longer constrained in the span of its years by the life and cycle of a biological organism, such a kind of life could live forever.[21]

Given that technology, though a doubtful deity, can be a wonderfully useful tool, how can we decide on its proper use to enable human flourishing? Christianity has had a mixed history in relation to scientific progress. We have already seen how many scientific pioneers were believers, but Christians have throughout history resisted many new advances from Stevenson's Rocket to Simpson's discovery of general anaesthesia (the latter opposed on the grounds that it countered the biblical curse that women would give birth in pain[22] (Gen. 3:16)). Well might Ted Peters complain that the stereotypical, knee-jerk Christian response is, 'We say, "No." And we add, "We say no because God says no."'[23]

However, the technology that was misused at Babel also enabled Noah to build the ark (Gen. 6), but both his motivation and purpose were entirely different: to save mankind rather than make a name for it. Similarly, biotechnology can save us from much unnecessary suffering and disability and should be welcomed as a gift from God if the means to achieve such goals are compatible with scriptural principles.

Leonardo vs Lego

In his Christian classic of bioethics, *Matters of Life and Death*, Professor John Wyatt delineates two distinct models of biotechnology which illustrate the second biblical limit on it:

> The Mark I human model is not the only one in town. We can improve things; we have the technology. I shall call this the 'Lego kit' view of the human body. There is nothing 'natural' about a Lego kit. There is no right or wrong way to put the pieces together. There is no master plan from the designers. There is no ethical basis of Lego construction. You can do what you like. In fact, as it says in the adverts, 'the only limitation is your own imagination'.[24]

In contrast to this, Wyatt illustrates another model:

> 'How much is the Mona Lisa worth, and is it worth more or less than the roof of the Sistine Chapel?' There can be no answer, because the value of a supreme masterpiece is incalculable and incommensurable. In place of the Lego-kit view of humanity, then, we have what I will call the *flawed masterpiece* view of humanity. Yes, the masterpiece may get defaced, it may decay from old age, the varnish may be cracked and yellowed, the frame may be riddled with woodworm. But through the imperfections we can still perceive a masterpiece.[25]

If the first limit on biotechnology is that it should not be worshipped, the second limit is the borderline between restoration of the masterpiece of humanity and reworking into a new species – fashioning a master-race of *techno sapiens*.[26] The scope of the various forms of transhumanism is vast, but is most obvious in the world-wide clamour for cloning.

Send in the Clones?

Though many countries have introduced a ban on human cloning, several mammals have already been cloned since Dolly the sheep became the first in 1997, and it is likely to be only a matter of time before a human clone is born. The potential benefits are obvious: to produce spare body parts that would not be rejected when transplanted, to 'replace' lost or dying children with a genetically-identical child, and to enable immortality – at least of one's genes.

The means are important, however. Producing tissue which will not be rejected is a worthy goal. It is likely to be achievable by using adult stem cells,[27] whereas sacrificing human embryos to obtain such cells is unacceptable to many Christians. Other goals of cloning clearly run counter to the revealed nature of humanity in the Bible, regardless of the means. Mortality is part of the human condition: 'It is destined that each person dies only once and after that comes judgment' (Heb. 9:27). To try to attain immortality is unequivocally in the 'Lego kit' camp. There are other, less obvious aspects of the fabric of God's universe that are violated by cloning: it threatens identity and individuality (in a way that the problems experienced by some identical twins give only the slightest hint of); it 'represents a blatant violation of the inner meaning of parent-child relations';[28] and it challenges the whole meaning of sexual reproduction, to name but a few. It is only if we hold fast to the bedrock of a biblical understanding of human beings that we will avoid humanity being washed away by the tide of well-meaning, but misplaced, technological totalitarianism.

Incarnation Secures Salvation

The incarnation of Jesus Christ entails both implications and consequences which relate to biotechnology and its application. The coming of Jesus as a man is a turning point of history. The fact that Christ 'appeared in a body' (1 Tim. 3:16) and has 'come in the flesh' (1 Jn. 4:2; 2 Jn. 7) is central to the theology of the New Testament.

It was necessary that the 'Word [Jesus] became flesh' (Jn. 1:14, NIV) so that he could be the 'second Adam' (Rom. 5:15–19; 1 Cor. 15:45–49) who would die for our sins, bringing us salvation from the penalty of sin we inherit from the 'first Adam'. Only Jesus could do this, and, 'There is no other name in all of heaven for people to call on to save them' (Acts 4:12).

Biotechnology, however, is ever ready to usurp this role, promising salvation from the curse of our human limitations and offering the promise of eternal life. Alcor, an organization in Arizona, has for a long time been offering the possibility of freezing the body at death to await the time when biotechnology will be in a position to revive it. They argue that the frozen corpse is not 'dead', merely in an analogous state to someone who has just had a cardiac arrest.[29] Alcor is a striking example of the emergence of biotechnology as a religious movement. It gives much of its webspace to justifying its position theologically. Likewise, the American Dr Richard Seed, who intends to clone children for childless couples, maintains that, 'God intended for man to become one with God . . . cloning and the reprogramming of DNA is the first step in becoming one with God.'[30]

However, as we have seen, the line between a legitimate desire to become *one with* God and a desire to *be* God can be a very fine one. We have to ask of any biotechnology, 'What is its spirituality?' Alastair McIntosh suggests that one spirituality acid test is to ask:

> 'Does this science optimally benefit the poor?' Anything short of a resounding 'Yes', anything that smacks of science in the absence of social justice, is corrupt.[31]

One suspects that both Alcor and Dr Seed are primarily concerned with the rich who can afford to pay for the immortality they hope to offer. It makes quite a contrast with the free gift of eternal life which Christ offers (Rom. 5:15–16,21).

Incarnation defines the limits of humanity

In the incarnation,

> God reveals himself as *a human being* – a Mark I, original human model. Christians treat the human body with special respect. Why? Because this strange and idiosyncratic collection of 100 000 genes, 10 billon nerve cells, several miles of wiring, 8 metres of intestinal plumbing, 5 litres of blood and assorted biochemical engineering – this is the form in which God became flesh.[32]

The Bible celebrates the (albeit flawed) masterpiece of our body as 'a temple of the Holy Spirit' (1 Cor. 6:19) just as Jesus regarded his own body as a temple (John 2:19,21). Jesus is both 'God with us' (Is. 7:14) and is one of us. As he 'has been with us in the darkness of the womb, he will be with us in the darkness of the tomb'.[33]

The transhumanist movement, however, rejects the view that human nature is a constant. On the contrary, 'Our duty, as men and women, is to proceed as if limits to our ability did not exist.'[34] The microchip, not biology, is our destiny,[35] and the age of the Mark I human is now drawing to a close. There are no 'absolute demarcations between our bodily existence and computer simulation.'[36] One day our brains will simply be uploaded into machines and 'we will be software, not hardware'.[37]

Such a vision of the future sits very uncomfortably with a faith in which the strong are called to lay down their lives for the weak. It seems far removed from a God whose 'power works best in [our] weakness' (2 Cor. 12:9). The paradox of the transhumanist vision of an enhanced mankind is that it will ultimately, 'redefine normality as defect and ultimately devalue the created self'.[38]

The incarnation gives a new perspective on suffering

Biotechnology promises to free us from suffering and pain – new antibiotics to overcome bacterial resistance, transplants and prosthetics to replace worn out body parts, vaccines to prevent HIV and cancers, and cloning and cryopreservation to ultimately cheat death itself.

Research using embryonic stem cells promises cures for diseases ranging from Alzheimer's to Parkinson's. There is often an intrinsic appeal to 'self-evident' moral imperatives. How can it be wrong when the outcome is so good? Some Christians support such arguments, utilizing, for example, Francis Bacon's idea that by scientific endeavour we can return to the state of perfection of the Garden of Eden before the Fall:

> The Baconian confidence believes that a perfect condition of nature is knowable, that nature has deviated from perfection, and that technology's mandate is to restore it to the right order.[39]

A superficial consideration of the incarnation may also appear to support this line of thinking. Clearly the relief of human suffering was a priority in the ministry of Jesus: 'Jesus travelled throughout Galilee teaching . . . preaching . . . And he healed people who had every kind of sickness and disease' (Mt. 4:23). Matthew even links Jesus healing 'all the sick' with Isaiah's prophecy of his incarnation: 'He took our sicknesses and removed our diseases' (Mt. 8:17). Jesus also commanded his followers to heal sick people (Mk. 16:18), and surely genetic research and biotechnology fall within the remit of this command?

Indeed it does, but only within the broader framework in which Jesus' own healing ministry was located. Jesus stated that the prime aim of his Incarnation was to 'seek and save those . . . who are lost' (Lk. 19:10). His mission was one of saving the souls of men and women, and his physical healings were a sign of his authority and ability to do this very thing (Mk. 2:9,10). There can be no more graphic illustration of the primacy of the spiritual over the physical in the priorities of Jesus than his saying in the Sermon on the Mount that, 'Itis better for you to lose one part of your body than for your whole body to be thrown into hell' (Mt. 5:30).

The obsession of twenty-first century society with leisure, comfort, and immunity from pain or hardship is in complete contrast to Jesus' first priority. He says this is to 'make the Kingdom of God your primary concern' (Mt. 6:33) – a priority which if taken seriously is more likely to lead into suffering of one kind or another than to be totally free from it (1 Peter 2:21). This does not mean that we adopt a 'martyr complex', but rather that we recognise that total freedom from human limitations is only to be found when the Kingdom of God comes in all its fullness, and is not to be sought in being uploaded into some cyborg immortality.

Playing God or Serving God?

The biblical world view is radically different from one that starts from the premise that 'atoms, chance and randomness' are all there is to guide us in our understanding of the universe. The Bible tells us that, 'everything comes from him; everything exists by his power and is intended for his glory' (Rom. 11:36) – and this must include biotechnology. However, we are to use the resources that God has given to us, not in order to 'play God', but to serve our neighbour. Both the failure to innovate (Mt. 25:14–30) and the failure to humble ourselves to meet others' needs where we can (Mt. 25:31–46) incur God's judgement. Sloth and pride are equally culpable.

The mandate to use technological innovation to enhance the quality of life for all is to be pursued within the boundaries which God sets:

> Let me underscore: an ethical use of technology would be obedient to biblical law, motivated by biblical love and measured by biblical justice.[40]

Interestingly, as Sas points out, these three scriptural requirements mirror the main historical schools of western ethical thought: the deontological or Kantian view, virtue ethics and utilitarianism respectively.[41] Within such liberal boundaries, we are free to explore (and indeed to play) with God in understanding and innovating in the wonderful universe he has given us. But, as in Eden, so today we must always remember:

> The good things that men do, can be made complete only by the things they refuse to do.[42]

Notes

[1] Ronald Cole-Turner, 'Science, Technology and Mission' in Max Stackhouse, Tim Dearborn and Scott Paeth (eds.), *The Local Church in a Global Era: Reflections for a New Century* (Eerdmans, 2000) p. 101

[2] Kerby Anderson, 'Technological Challenges of the 21st Century' – www.probe.org/content/view/894/171/

[3] Peter Hodgson, *Christianity and Science* (Oxford University Press, 1990) p. 26

[4] In Maxwell's day, of course, it was the King James Version of the Bible which was used, so the inscription actually reads, 'The works of the Lord are great, sought out of all them that have pleasure therein.'

[5] Ian Barbour, *Issues in Science and Religion* (SCM Press, 1966) p. 222

[6] R. Hooykaas, *Religion and the Rise of Modern Science* (Scottish Academic Press, 1972) p. 12

[7] Nigel M. de S. Cameron, 'Christian vision for the biotech century' in Charles Colson and Nigel M. de S. Cameron (eds.), *Human Dignity and the Biotech Century* (IVP, 2004) p. 27

[8] Vinoth Ramachandra, *The Gods That Fail* (Paternoster, 1996) p. 66

[9] Helga Kuhse and Peter Singer *Should the Baby Live?; The Problem of Handicapped Infants* (Oxford University Press,

1985); Jonathan Glover *Causing Death and Saving Lives* (Pan, 1997)

10 'I teach you the overman. Man is something that is to be overcome' (Friedrich Nietzsche, *Thus Spake Zarathustra* (The Modern Library, 1995) p. 12

11 Kevin Warwick, 'Cyborg 1.0' in *Wired*, Issue 8.02, February 2000, p. 145 –

www.wired.com/wired/archive/8.02/warwick.html

12 Transhuman is shorthand for 'transitional human'. Transhumanism is the development of human beings physically and intellectually through the use of technology. For more information see www.wikipedia.org/wiki/Transhumanism and the website of the World Transhumanist Association – www.transhumanism.org

13 Daryl Sas, 'Reliance on Technology: Stem Cell Research and Beyond' in John Frederic Kilner, C. Christopher Hook and Diane B. Uustal (eds.), *Cutting Edge Bioethics* (Eerdmans, 2002) p. 86

14 John Calvin, *Commentary on Genesis 1554* (Banner of Truth, 1965)

15 Rene Dubos, *A God Within* (Sphere, 1976) p. 115

16 Karl Rahner, *Theological Investigations vol IX: Writings of 1965–7* (Herder and Herder, 1972) pp. 205–252

17 Charles Curran. 'The Contraceptive Revolution and the Human Condition' in Stephen Lammers and Allen Verhey (eds.), *On Moral Medicine* (Eerdmans, 1987) p. 319

18 Philip Hefner, *Technology and Human Becoming* (Fortress Press, 2003)

19 Stephen Garner, 'Hacking the Divine' – www.greenflame. org/docs/Garner-HackingtheDivine.pdf

20 Thomas Traherne, quoted in David Atkinson, *The Message of Genesis 1–11* (IVP, 1990) p. 43

21 Richard Jastrow, *The Enchanted Loom: Mind in the Universe* (Simon and Schuster, 1984) p. 166–167

22 Roy Porter, *Blood and Guts: A Short History of Medicine* (Allen Lane, 2002) p. 124

23 Ted Petera, 'Cloning Shock: A Theological Reaction' in Ronald Cole-Turner (ed.) *Human Cloning: Religious*

Responses (Westminster John Knox Press, 1997) p. 16

24 John Wyatt, *Matters of Life and Death* (IVP, 1998) p. 31

25 Wyatt, *Matters of Life and Death*, p. 55

26 C. Christopher Hook, 'Techno Sapiens' in Colson and Cameron, *Human Dignity and the Biotech Century*, pp. 75–97

27 Neil Scolding, 'New Cells from Old' in *Lancet* 2001 No. 357, pp. 329–330

28 Leon Kass and James Wilson, *The Ethics of Human Cloning* (American Enterprise Institute, 1998) p. 27

29 www.alcor.org

30 Quoted in Alistair McIntosh, 'The Cult of Biotechnology' – www.alastairmcintosh.com/articles/1998_biotechnology.htm

31 McIntosh, 'The Cult of Biotechnology'

32 Wyatt, *Matters of Life and Death*, p. 69

33 Gilbert Meilaender, *Bioethics: a Primer for Christians* (Paternoster, 1999) p. 30

34 Pierre Teilhard de Chardin – www.wikiquote.org/wiki/Pierre_Teilhard_de_Chardin

35 Bart Kosko, *The Fuzzy Future: From Society and Science to Heaven in a Chip* (Harmony, 1999) p. 256

36 N. Katherine Hayles, *How We Became Posthuman; Virtual Bodies in Cybernetics* (University of Chicago Press, 1999) pp. 2–3

37 Ray Kurzweil, *The Age of Spiritual Machines* (Viking, 1999) p. 129

38 Mark Hanson, 'Indulging Anxiety: Human Enhancement from a Protestant Perspective' in *Christian Bioethics* 1999, No. 5, pp. 121–138

39 Ronald Cole-Turner, 'Science, Technology and Mission' in Max Stackhouse, Tim Dearborn and Scott Paeth (eds.), *The Local Church in a Global Era: Reflections for a New Century* (Eerdmans, 2000) p. 156

40 Daryl Sas, 'Reliance on Technology: Stem Cell Research and Beyond', p. 87

[41] The deontological approach to ethics stresses moral obligations arising out of duty and the rights of others. Virtue ethics focus on what kind of person one should try to be. Utilitarian approaches to ethics are concerned only with the consequences of actions. For more information, see www.wikipedia.org/wiki/Deontological, www.wikipedia.org/wiki/Virtue_ethics and www.wikipedia.org/wiki/Utilitarianism

[42] Paul Ramsey quoted in Kass and Wilson, *The Ethics of Human Cloning*, p. 59

Some believe people are judged by the way they live life, and others by the way they leave it.

Mary Alice in *Desperate Housewives*

3. Killing Me Softly

Tony Watkins

Two of the film highlights of 2004 were *Vera Drake* and *Million Dollar Baby*. Both of them were intelligent, superbly crafted Oscar nominees, and both were deeply heart-wrenching as they thoughtfully explored major ethical issues. While one is all about an ordinary, caring woman 'helping young girls out' in the days when abortion was illegal, the other focuses on a man who finally has to wrestle with the decision of whether to end the life of a paralysed young woman. Few readers of this book would ever be in a place where they might face the prospect of being personally involved in acts of abortion or euthanasia, of course. But the issues involved touch the lives of many of us, whether it be family members whose suffering we wish was over, or friends who have abortions, even if they never tell us.

Vera Drake

Vera Drake was another gritty masterpiece by British writer/director Mike Leigh. Leigh has been making

films set in the British working classes since directing
Bleak Moments in 1971. With his devotion to low-budget
films using British actors, he has developed a reputation
for making bleakly realistic 'kitchen sink dramas'. Some
people criticise him, however, for patronising working
class people, trading in stereotypes and caricatures. He
resists this strongly, saying, 'Actually, the last thing my
characters are is stereotypes because they are far too
specific and idiosyncratic, like we all are, to be able to
qualify in a million years as stereotypes.'[1]

Vera (Imelda Staunton in the performance of her
career) herself may be seen as stereotypical in some
ways – but far from it in others. She is a char lady in
Islington in 1950. It is no surprise that she exemplifies
everything we associate with British post-war spirit. She
is constantly cheerful despite the difficulties of life just
five years after the war. It is a time of rising optimism,
but rationing is still in place and money is tight, so
luxuries are unthinkable. Husband Stan (Phil Davis)
works for his brother Frank (Adrian Scarborough) in a
garage. Frank is doing well and has risen to the middle
classes, living in the suburbs, running a car and able to
afford a washing machine. His wife Joyce is unsatisfied
and wants more, but Vera is content looking after her
family, working as a cleaner to help make ends meet,
and dropping in on elderly neighbours to make sure
they are alright and to make them a cup of tea. While
Vera and Stan's son Sid (Daniel Mays) is confident
and ebullient, with a zest for life, daughter Ethel (Alex
Kelly), by contrast, is a social misfit – not very bright
and painfully shy. Any hope of her marrying seems like
wishful thinking until Vera invites the equally diffident
Reg (Eddie Marsan) home for tea with the family.
Gradually, Ethel and Reg develop a restrained fondness
for each other, and they become engaged.

But while all of this conventional, post-war working class life is going on, Vera has a secret; even Stan has not the slightest inkling of it. Sean O'Hagan writes that: 'Much of the film's cumulative power lies in its delineation of a rock solid family suddenly rocked to the core by a revelation that is literally beyond their comprehension.'[2] While everybody knows how public spirited Vera is, there is only one person who knows that she takes her sense of duty into the realm of the criminal: Lily (Ruth Sheen), the woman whom the girls approach to make arrangements for their abortions – secretly, of course, since legalised abortion is still nearly two decades away. Vera knows that what she is doing is criminal – just over a century earlier, she would have faced the death penalty or exile – but it is not the fear of prosecution which has made her keep it quiet for decades. Mike Leigh gives the reason why:

> To protect her family. Not herself. Vera's not ashamed of what she does, but she knows the pain and ignominy it will bring. They don't need to know, basically. Plus, as her husband says, had he known about it, he would have put a stop to it.[3]

She knows that the rest of her family will not see the issue in the same way as her. For them, it is dirty and shameful, as well as criminal. For them, the principle of the matter is more important than each individual situation. For them, the traditional Christian understanding of the sanctity of life is unshakeable. But for Vera, it is an act of compassion – a duty of care which is not essentially different from looking in on the house-bound or inviting the lonely to tea. And she approaches the task in the same kind of chirpy, matter-of-fact way. Vera is relentlessly cheerful as she bustles about, smiling, humming, encouraging, caring and just passing the time of day while she syringes soapy water into a woman's womb.

Everything about Vera speaks of deep contentment. She's happy with her family, her friends, her life. She is not in the least bit envious of Frank and Joyce's new luxuries. She has everything she wants and she is glad to help others in any way she can – including inducing a miscarriage for someone whose life is about to fall apart because of an unplanned pregnancy. She doesn't even take payment. In fact, Vera is so positive about everybody else that it never enters her head that Lily *does* get paid by the girls, but never passes a penny of it to Vera. Mike Leigh wants us to feel that Vera is thoroughly good-hearted, and that she does what she does for the best possible motives. And the same motives – care for others, wanting to spare them shame and disgrace – is what stops her ever breathing a word of it to Stan. Peter Bradshaw writes:

> Vera's vocation as an abortionist exists entirely within the concentric circles of criminal concealment and euphemistic taboo. It is not merely that it is a secret from the authorities: it is a secret from Vera herself. She has no language to describe what she does or reflect on it in any way. The closest she comes to telling the miserable women what will happen to them after their appallingly dangerous treatment is to say that they will soon get a pain 'down below', at which point they should go to the lavatory and 'it will come away'. So when one of these women is taken to hospital almost dying in agony, and poor respectable Vera is confronted by the police, she is as hapless and hopeless as her victim-patients, with no way of defending or explaining herself. Her only response is mutely to absorb unimaginable quantities of shame.[4]

The two-minute scene in which Vera tries to tell Stan why she has been arrested, but can only manage to sob 'I'm sorry', before finally whispering the truth into his ear, and then sobbing again as Stan looks stupefied, is as moving a scene as there is in cinema. Stunned though he is, he understands what drove her:

> **Sid:** How could she do that?
> **Stan:** She was trying to help people out, Sid.
> **Sid:** It's wrong, though.
> **Stan:** Well, whatever she done, she done it out the kindness of her heart.
> **Sid:** She's let us down.
> **Stan:** [firmly] No.

Although reviewer James Mottram, writes, 'it is left to the audience to sieve through the rights and wrongs of Vera's actions,'[5] Mike Leigh's sympathetic portrayal of Vera strongly suggests that he thinks she is right to act in the way she does.

Million Dollar Baby

Million Dollar Baby seems to be more ambivalent on the big ethical issue. Perhaps part of the reason for this is that, in contrast to *Vera Drake*, the majority of the film does not revolve around that one issue, although it comes to dominate at the end. *Million Dollar Baby* is, arguably, Clint Eastwood's finest hour as a director. Although *Vera Drake* seems to have been shunned at the 2005 Oscars, having previously won three Golden Globes, Eastwood was nevertheless a worthy winner for Best Director. Paul Haggis wrote the screenplay based on two short stories from *Rope Burns: Stories from the*

Corner by former boxing manager and 'cut man' Jerry Boyd (under the pseudonym of F.X. Toole).

It tells the story of veteran boxing trainer/manager Frankie Dunn (Clint Eastwood) and Maggie Fitzgerald (Hilary Swank), a young woman who turns up at his gym wanting Frankie to train her. He refuses to even consider the idea of her using his gym – she's a girl. But when Frankie's right-hand man Eddie 'Scrap-Iron' Dupris (Morgan Freeman) tells him that she has paid six months' dues, he concedes to her training in the gym, but refuses to give her any help. These three characters are at least as stereotypical as anything in *Vera Drake:* Frankie is gruff, cautious and deeply-scarred emotionally, but a great trainer; Maggie admits she is 'trash', but is single minded in her determination to make something of her life by becoming a boxer; Scrap is an old ex-boxer who has fallen on hard times, and who provides the gravelly, compassionate voice of wisdom.

It is Scrap, of course, who gently encourages Maggie late in the evening after everyone else has left the gym, while Frankie tells Maggie that she is wasting her time – she's starting to train too late in life to ever be a success. Late one evening, Frankie discovers her still practising at the gym. She tells him that she is celebrating her birthday, and fills him in on her background – waitressing since she was thirteen, a brother in prison, a sister cheating the welfare system, an obese mother – and says: 'The problem is, this is the only thing I ever felt good doing. If I'm too old for this, then I got nothing. That enough truth to suit you?' Frankie relents and starts to train her. Scrap's voiceover reflects that:

> All fighters are pig-headed one way or another. Some part of them always thinks they know better than you about

something. . . . Truth is, even if they're wrong, even if that one thing is going to be the ruin of them, if you can beat that last bit out of them, then they're not fighters at all.

It is a reflection that hangs questioningly over the final sequences of the film. Maggie finally gets her shot at contending for the world championship title. The reigning champion is known for her foul play, and Frankie insists that Maggie protect herself at all times. After being beaten hard early on in the bout, Maggie begins to turn the tables, but when the referee sends the boxers to their corners, she turns away. Her opponent hits Maggie hard on the side of the head, sending her flying to the ground – but her stool had just been placed into the ring. Frankie lunges to pull it away before Maggie falls on it, but too late. She hits it and is paralysed from the neck down.

Frankie ensures that she gets the best possible care and stays with her for most of each day over the ensuing months. It is clear that Maggie has become very dear to him – a substitute for the daughter from whom he is estranged. He also feels some responsibility for what happened, since he had made it possible. However, after Maggie's leg is amputated, her despair grows deeper. One evening, she asks Frankie to do for her what her father had done for his sick dog. 'Don't even think about that,' Frankie says. Maggie pleads:

I can't be like this, Frankie. Not after what I've done. I've seen the world. People chanted my name. . . . You think I ever dreamed that'd happen? I was born 2 lb 1½ oz. Daddy used to tell me I fought to get into this world and I'd fight my way out. That's all I want to do, Frankie. I just don't want to fight you to do it. I got what I needed. I got it all. Don't let 'em keep taking it away from me.

Don't let me lie here till I can't hear those people chanting no more.

Frankie refuses but is woken in the middle of the night by the phone ringing – Maggie has bitten her tongue to try to bleed to death. It's too much for him. Later, Scrap sees Frankie pack some syringes into his bag and seems to subtly encourage him that he's doing the right thing:

People die every day, Frankie – mopping floors, washing dishes. And you know what their last thought is? 'I never got my shot.' Because of you, Maggie got her shot. If she dies today, you know what her last thought will be? 'I think I did alright.' I know I could rest with that.

Eyes on the Prize

On what basis do Frankie and Vera make their moral decisions about the rightness of what they do? Frankie's approach to ethics is *consequentialist* – he only thinks about the end result, the consequences for Maggie. He is, of course, motivated by a deep sense of care for Maggie. He cannot bear to see her in distress and helpless. While she tells Scrap that 'it doesn't hurt at all', she is in emotional anguish, and Frankie wants to put an end to her suffering.

However, the fact that Frankie only considers Maggie – and that, however understandably, Maggie only considers herself – shows the inadequacies with consequentialist thinking. It is too hard to assess what the full consequences of an action will be. He does not anticipate the consequences for himself particularly well. The priest Father Horvak (Brian O'Byrne) does, however, recognising that Frankie is already weighed down by guilt that he doesn't know how to deal with:

> Frankie, I've seen you at Mass almost every day for twenty-three years. The only person that comes to church that much is the kind that can't forgive himself for something. Whatever sins you're carrying – they're nothing compared to this. Forget about God or heaven or hell, if you do this thing, you'll be lost – somewhere so deep you'll never find yourself again.

Father Horvak's point seems to be not that the sin of killing Maggie is in itself unforgivable, but that Frankie is in a place – and has been for a very long time – where he can't seek forgiveness. This, surely, is what lies behind the conversations between Frankie and the priest earlier in the film in which he questions the idea of the Trinity and other doctrines. Clearly, after years of this, the priest's patience is wearing thin, but by failing to take Frankie's questions seriously, he has never been able to help deal with the deeper issues. Frankie can't find forgiveness because, it would seem, the church has never helped him to see that full forgiveness is all from God's grace. The lack of clarity about the gospel means that he has never moved on from baiting the priest each day. And yet, he can't let faith go altogether – he goes to Mass each day, which does suggest a deeper hunger than simply wanting to give Father Horvak a hard time, and he does pray at night. It's a simple, unconfident prayer:

> Well, do your best, Lord, to protect Katy. Annie too. Other than that, you know what I want. There's no use me repeating myself.

One feels that Frankie might well echo the cry of the father in Mark 9:24 – 'I do believe, but help me not to doubt!' So for more than two decades, Frankie has been carrying a burden of guilt, instinctively knowing that the resolution to this is found only in the Christian faith, yet failing to find it in the Christian church. Father Horvak does at least realise that if Frankie has still not been able to deal with the earlier guilt (for what we don't know, other than that it is connected with the estrangement of his daughter and, perhaps, of his wife), he will be even less able to deal with the guilt of killing someone – even if it is motivated by deep compassion.

But Frankie feels that there is no right answer, saying, 'it's committing a sin by doing it. By keeping her alive I'm killing her. Know what I mean? How do I get around that?' So, feeling that he can't win either way, he acts on the basis of the consequences for Maggie – an end to her misery. Scrap reflects:

> He gave her a single shot. There was enough adrenaline to do the job a few times over. He didn't want her going through this again. Then he walked out. I don't think he had anything left. I went back to the gym, figuring he'd turn up sooner or later. . . . Frankie never came back at all. Frankie didn't leave a note and nobody knew where he went. . . . I just hope he found someplace where he could find a little peace. . . . But that's probably wishful thinking.

It seems that Frankie may well have even lost the ability to keep on fighting to achieve reconciliation with his daughter. But as well as the consequences for Frankie himself, everyone else in his and Maggie's orbit also has consequences to bear, not least Scrap who has lost two friends and is left holding the baby with the gym. Was there really no alternative to euthanasia?

The Good Life

Vera Drake may also be working on consequentialist thinking. Like Frankie Dunn, she gives little thought to the personal consequences for herself, thinking only of the benefits for the girls she 'helps out'. She is concerned to spare them from shame or from hardship. But this concern, as we have already seen, is powerfully presented as entirely consistent with the rest of her life. So maybe Vera's ethical basis is not consequentialism but *virtue ethics* in which the focus is not on outcomes, but on what kind of person one ought to be. The goal of virtue ethics is *eudaimonia*, which means flourishing or success – living a full, happy and good life. Aristotle maintained that only an older person with a rich experience of life could achieve this. To reach this goal requires developing virtues such as kindness, compassion, generosity, courage, honesty, justice and friendliness. These virtues are all very much a part of Vera's life. As Frank says to Stan, 'She's got a heart of gold, that woman.' 'She's a diamond,' Stan agrees.

Leigh seems to be implying that, in stark contrast with this fundamentally good woman, the social system and the law were anything but good. He criticises the society of the day for valuing outward respectability above everything else, and for the inequality between working class and middle class people who were able to use their connections and money to procure an abortion on the grounds of protecting the woman's mental health (legitimate grounds since a landmark court case in 1938[6]). It seems clear that Leigh is also highly critical of the law at the time. The film's sympathies are obviously with Vera, and with the women who are 'in trouble'. It suggests that Vera is right to do what she does because abortion is the obvious solution to their difficulties, and no other options are open to them. Perhaps, then, Leigh is a consequentialist after all, since the desired end result is the termination of their pregnancies, and, therefore, also of their shame. Since back-street abortions are so risky and, as one doctor in *Vera Drake* says, 'must be stopped', the implication is that it was right to change the law in 1967. All these women should have access to the standards of clinical care experienced by middle-class Susan Wells (Sally Hawkins) who is able to pay a hundred guineas for her abortion.

Once again, though, the wider consequences are ignored. While Leigh shows the distress of some of the girls at the time of their abortions, he only shows two negative consequences of Vera's secret life. One was the drastic consequences for Pamela Barnes, the young woman who became infected; the other was Vera's arrest and conviction, and the impact on her family. But there is nothing here to suggest that there are any long-term impacts of abortion. In reality, the emotional trauma can continue for years – a lifetime even. Naomi Wolf interviewed women about their sexual experiences for her book *Promiscuities* and says: 'Out of all the difficult sexual events the women experienced, it was the abortions alone that seemed, even twenty years later, just too painful to integrate ...'[7] John Wyatt, in his *Matters of Life and Death*, quotes some experiences of some women as revealed in the *Evening Standard* in 1996. One said, 'I told no one at the time of my abortion and never have since. Many women block it out of their minds. They are the lucky ones. I don't regret it but I know that I will feel stigmatised for the rest of my life.' Another admits that, 'The image of that room still haunts me.' Another comments that she was at first elated, then depressed and says: 'I know this is pathetic, but I feel that if I don't get pregnant [with her new boyfriend] it will be a punishment.'[8]

A Bigger Picture

Wyatt also talks about the implications of abortion for society as a whole. He writes:

> Does it make no difference to me what practical decisions you make about the ultimate value of life, and *vice versa*? Is society just a collection of private individuals all doing their own thing? The very fact that disabled people like Tom Shakespeare and Christy Nolan want to protest against the abortion of affected fetuses is evidence that this is an inadequate view of society and of the value of human life. It seems to me that the liberal individualistic concept of society as a series of autonomous individuals is a modern mythical construction. It does not fit with reality and it does not fit with our deepest human intuitions.[9]

The same arguments apply to the question of euthanasia. The ending of a life reverberates out through society since the individuals most closely affected will bear some emotional scars. These will inevitably affect interactions with others – especially in the way that others are valued. Once a decision has been taken that one particular life has such low value that it can be cut short, the value of many other lives is called into question. Such relativising of the value of a human life impacts on everyone in the society, whether or not they are directly affected.

The Christian view has always been that human life has immense value. A human, whether fetal or adult, may not be rational and self-conscious, but that does not mean they are of no value. It sees humans only in terms of their abilities, their usefulness. The biblical understanding is that all humans are made in the image of God. That has always driven Christians to great compassion for the vulnerable – for the unborn child, for the disabled, for the young woman in great distress because of an unwanted pregnancy, for the dying. Christians are not oblivious to consequences, but our view of society as an interdependent whole stops us seeing them in such a narrow view as Frankie Dunn. Christians, like Vera, are concerned about what kind of person we ought to be – but what we ought to be is like God: full of compassion for fetus as well as mother. Christians also make ethical decisions on the basis of a third approach: *deontological* ethics which stresses the importance of principles and duty. As Christ's representatives, we have a responsibility to live according to the ethical principles God has given us in Scripture. Both Frankie's and Vera's decisions were partly prompted because the people concerned did not want to be dependent on others for their care. But John Wyatt stresses that we were made to be mutually dependent. He quotes Gilbert Meilander:

> We are dependent beings, and to think otherwise – to make independence our project, however sincerely – is to live a lie, to fly in the face of reality.[10]

Notes

[1] Quoted by Sean O'Hagan, 'I'm allowed to do what I want – that amazes me', *The Observer*, 5 December 2005 – film. guardian.co.uk/interview/interviewpages/0,6737,1366515,00.html

[2] Sean O'Hagan, 'I'm allowed to do what I want – that amazes me'

[3] Sean O'Hagan, 'I'm allowed to do what I want – that amazes me'

[4] Peter Bradshaw, 'Vera Drake', *The Guardian*, 7 January 2005 – film.guardian.co.uk/News_Story/Critic_Review/Guardian_Film_of_the_week/0,4267,1384377,00.html

[5] James Mottram, 'Vera Drake', Channel 4.com – www.channel4.com/film/reviews/film.jsp?id=136249&page=1

[6] In 1938, gynaecologist Aleck Bourne was tried for performing an abortion on a fourteen-year-old girl who had been raped by some soldiers in London. The judge said that the jury was entitled to take the view that Bourne was essentially acting to preserve the life of the mother. The jury acquitted him, but in 1966 Bourne became a founder of the Society for the Protection of Unborn Children because he was appalled that his case was being used to justify what became the 1967 Abortion Act which, effectively, allowed abortion on demand. For more on this, see John Wyatt, *Matters of Life and Death* (IVP, 1998) p. 126; 'Obituary: Mr Aleck Bourne – An eminent gynaecologist', *The Times*, 30 December 1974 – www.stuart.n.clarke.btinternet.co.uk/AddlMatObitBourne.html

[7] Naomi Wolf, *Promiscuities* (Chatto and Windus, 1997) p. 197

[8] John Wyatt, *Matters of Life and Death* (IVP, 1998) p. 129

[9] Wyatt, *Matters of Life and Death*, p. 139

[10] Gilbert Meilander, *Bioethics: A Primer for Christians* (Paternoster Press, 1997) p. 59, quoted in Wyatt, *Matters of Life and Death*, p. 59

I gave them the wrong warning. I should have told them to run as fast as they can, run and hide because the monsters are coming – the human race.

The Doctor in *Doctor Who: The Christmas Invasion*

4. Paddling in the Gene Pool

Caroline Puntis

If I were the biblical God I would be very annoyed. He made the thing and saw that it was good. And now people are scribbling all over the artwork.
Margaret Atwood[1]

As a novelist, Canadian writer Margaret Atwood is familiar with the concept of playing God. She frequently ventures into another time period to create her worlds, inevitably drawing upon her worries in the here and now for inspiration. She sees this task as being similar to that of the scientist:

> Science and fiction both begin with similar questions: What if? Why? How does it all work? But they focus on different areas of life on earth. The experiments of science should be replicable, and those of literature should not be (why write the same book twice?).[2]

Oryx and Crake[3] follows in the footsteps of her earlier novel *The Handmaid's Tale*[4] in creating a futuristic dystopia in which the follies of modern man lead the

57

world into chaos. While *The Handmaid's Tale* followed the scenario in which mass infertility and religious fundamentalism leads to the subjection of women, *Oryx and Crake* focuses on the moral failings of scientists. Yet Atwood is not anti-science. She comments:

> Science is a way of knowing, and a tool. Like all ways of knowing, it can be turned to bad uses. And it can be bought and sold, and it often is. But it is not in itself bad. Like electricity, it's neutral.[5]

In spite of its setting towards the end of the twenty-first century, Atwood insists that her story is not science fiction – a term that she attributes more to 1930s bug-eyed monsters, rockets and chemicals. She also points out that science fiction is often a fantasy, with people flying around on dragons or meeting alien life forms. Her genre is more along the lines of George Orwell's *1984* and Aldous Huxley's *Brave New World*. She prefers to call this future-based writing 'speculative fiction', as it considers scenarios that are extrapolations of existing issues, rather than imagined ones. The background research for *Oryx and Crake* was inadvertently supplied:

> I'd been clipping small items from the back pages of newspapers for years, and noting with alarm that trends derided ten years ago as paranoid fantasies had become possibilities, then actualities.[6]

Brought up by an entomologist father, and with biologists and physicists in the family as well, Atwood is, in fact, a big fan of science. Her interest in learning more about species facing extinction has led her to fear for the preservation of the natural world – not least the human race itself.

Compounds and Chemicals

The 'what if' of *Oryx and Crake* is simply, What if we continue down the road we're already on? How slippery is the slope? What are our saving graces? Who's got the will to stop us?[7]

The world Atwood creates feels alarmingly plausible – a logical end to the means we have begun to employ in an attempt to improve our lives today. For example, in the here and now she sees pharmaceutical companies ready to make money out of the worldwide obsession with beauty and youth, but without thinking of the consequences. The market is saturated with money-spinning schemes: anti-ageing creams and products that claim to turn back the clock on fine lines; minor plastic surgery that can be performed in a lunch hour; constantly-changing advice on how to eat healthily and lose weight.

In the world of *Oryx and Crake*, America is divided into two domains: Compounds and pleeblands. The Compounds are where the scientific elite live with their families and work on the eternally-bankable products that claim to change people's lives for the better. The air is cleaner, people are safe and secure, and good things – authentic products such as real meat – are available. These mini cities embody utopian ideals to varying degrees, unlike the world beyond the gates known as the pleeblands – a world of crime, prostitution, drugs and disease. Compound-dwellers are more or less forbidden to go into the pleeblands because of their lack of immunity to infections, which could then be brought back inside. A *Big Brother*-style secret police force, CorpSeCorps, makes sure that everyone's movements are always accounted for, along with virtually all details of their personal lives.

Jimmy, the character at the centre of the novel, grew up in the Compounds, the son of two scientists. He remembers his father working on creating a pig – called a pigoon – with which it was possible to grow and harvest human organs for transplantation. Jimmy's father was willing to toe the party line, but his mother's faith in what they were doing failed. Having given up work, ostensibly to look after Jimmy, she eventually fled the Compound in order to join with those who still believed in 'making life better for people – not just people with money'. She attacks Jimmy's father, saying, 'there's research and there's research. What you're doing – the pig brain thing. You're interfering with the building blocks of life. It's immoral. It's . . . sacrilegious.'[8]

Jimmy, however, is no scientist but a man with a passion for words. At college, he writes a paper that eventually becomes his final dissertation: 'Self-Help Books of the Twentieth Century: Exploiting Hope and Fear'. For all the new products there is, of course, a prevailing culture of advertising, which continues to drive the whole machine of consumption. Jimmy cuts a career path in advertising that directs him into another Compound called AnooYoo. At his interview, the company's ethos is explained:

> 'What people want is perfection,' said the man. 'In themselves.'
>
> 'But they need the steps to be pointed out,' said the woman.
>
> 'In a simple order,' said the man.
>
> 'With encouragement,' said the woman. 'And a positive attitude.'
>
> 'They like to hear about the before and after,' said the man. 'It's the art of the possible. But with no guarantees, of course.'

'You showed great insight into the process,' the woman said. 'In your dissertation. We found it very mature.'

'If you know one century, you know them all,' said the man.[9]

For Atwood, the possibility of human progress seems to be an illusion. We are constantly engaged in the same battle as generations before us: how to halt, or at least slow down, the relentless march towards death. Whereas this has chiefly been a spiritual preoccupation in many cultures, the idea that we should be paying attention to our souls in consideration of some supposed afterlife is no longer very popular in western secularised society. We cannot know – in the scientific, rational manner to which we have become accustomed – what happens to us after our bodies are laid to rest. Therefore, it seems to make more sense to concentrate on what we think we know now, and make the most of what we have in the present. For the non-believer, today's 'spirituality' is often no more than a convenient way to disarm the stresses of modern living – it's all about now. For most people, the easiest way to achieve a sense of defeating time and climbing up towards perfection is through outward appearance. In Atwood's world, there is always a product available to hand:

AnooYoo was a collection of cesspool denizens who existed for no other reason than to prey on the phobias and void the bank accounts of the anxious and gullible ... Pills to make you fatter, thinner, hairier, balder, whiter, browner, blacker, yellower, sexier, and happier. It was [Jimmy's] task to describe and extol, to present the vision of what – oh, so easily! – could come to be. Hope and fear, desire and revulsion, these were his stocks-in-trade, on these he rang his changes.[10]

In Search of the Immortal

> 'Men can imagine their own deaths, they can see them
> coming, and the mere thought of impending death acts
> like an aphrodisiac ... human beings hope they can
> stick their souls into someone else, some new version
> of themselves, and live on forever.'
>
> 'As a species, we're doomed by hope, then?'
>
> 'You could call it hope. That, or desperation.'
>
> 'But we're doomed without hope, as well,' said
> Jimmy.
>
> 'Only as individuals,' said Crake cheerfully.[11]

Science is constantly trying to overtake us in the fast
lane when it comes to matters of death. In the western
world, we grow up believing that medicine can fix just
about anything, and when it fails we want our money
back. We can make ourselves fitter, healthier and more
pleasing to the eye – but we all must face death in
the end. To the young, this end often feels as though
it will never come. To the ageing, the end is, perhaps,
renegotiable if you buy the right products and give the
appearance of youth – forty is the new thirty, and so on.
But we cannot progress beyond the ultimate statistic –
one out of one dies, regardless of whatever false hopes
science and the media may have given us.

There is, no doubt, some truth in Atwood's idea that
having a child is another way to grab a piece of eternity.
She gleefully picks up her concerns for the morality
of reproduction in Jimmy's reflections on the process
– from his father's new girlfriend's point of view:

> No baby brother for him yet, she'd say, but they were still
> 'working on it'. He did not wish to visualise the hormone-
> sodden, potion-ridden, gel-slathered details of such work.
> If nothing 'natural' happened soon, she said, they'd try

'something else' from one of the agencies – Infantade, Foetility, Perfectababe, one of those . . . They'd have a few trial runs, and if the kids from those didn't measure up they'd recycle them for the parts, until at last they got something that fit all their specs – perfect in every way, not only a math whiz but beautiful as the dawn. They'd load this hypothetical wonderkid up with their bloated expectations until the poor tyke burst under the strain. Jimmy didn't envy him. (He envied him.)[12]

Reason declares that this must be the way forward: now that it is possible to choose the best genes for junior, why would I not choose the best possible start for him in life? Even Jimmy, who bears all of Atwood's cynicism and concerns that this is not the solution to the problems of the human race, feels drawn to the idea that, somehow, perfection could be achieved before you're even born. If you had every advantage in the beginning, surely this would make your life better? There is also the possibility that having a perfect child would, in some way, make the parents seem more perfect, bringing satisfaction on many levels.

Throughout *Oryx and Crake*, Atwood develops the connection between the longing for eternity and the longing for perfection. In the Bible, the two are inextricably linked: God and his ways are perfect;[13] he is the living God, the eternal King;[14] Jesus, once made perfect, became the source of eternal salvation.[15] Without a spiritual element, the question of how to truly satisfy these longings is a futile one. The writer of Ecclesiastes hits the nail on the head with his usual aplomb:

> I have thought about this in connection with the various kinds of work God has given people to do. God has made everything beautiful for its own time. He has planted eternity in the human heart, but even so, people cannot see the whole scope of God's work from beginning to end.[16]

Embracing the concept and reality of death must be the key to these verses; as the writer also states at the beginning of chapter three, 'There is a time for everything, a season for every activity under heaven. A time to be born and a time to die.'[17] The promise of eternity is not fulfilled in leaving part of ourselves behind to continue forever on earth. The eternal is a reality – one in which the Bible teaches us to hope. Ignoring this truth leaves man in a particularly woeful state: if hope must be satisfied here and now, and perfection is what we are hoping for, then, as Jimmy says, we are doomed.

Breaking the Line

> 'Immortality,' said Crake, 'is a concept. If you take "mortality" as being, not death, but the foreknowledge of it and the fear of it, then "immortality" is the absence of such fear. Babies are immortal. Edit out the fear and you'll be—'[18]

It is through the titular Crake that Atwood really lets her projected worldview take ultimate shape. Jimmy and Crake were at high school together in one of the Compounds. Together they surfed the Internet, played ultra-violent computer games and watched a variety of downloads such as porn, assisted suicides and beheadings from around the globe. One of Crake's favourite games was Extinctathon, in which contestants would battle for supreme knowledge of extinct animals, birds and plants. Crake took his name from an extinct Australian bird, the red-necked crake. One day, when the boys were surfing the Web looking at porn sites, they came across the image of a beautiful young Asian girl. Crake printed off a copy for them both. Jimmy tried hard to conceal his fascination, but he was hooked. The girl was perfect.

Crake was the brightest kid in the class. Having been headhunted by the best of academia, he went on to work for one of the most exclusive Compounds, RejoovenEsense. With the best brains in the country, this body-oriented centre has no trouble developing desirable products for the hoards of unsuspecting pleeblanders who are always willing to pay for their dreams to come true.

Years after their friendship seems to have fizzled out, Crake turns up on Jimmy's doorstep. Somehow he knows the truth that Jimmy himself has only just discovered: that Jimmy's estranged mother has been executed for treason. Crake obtains special passes and vaccines for them to make a casual visit to the pleeblands for some dirty pleasure. On New York's 'Street of Dreams' he explains that people come here from all over the world to shop around for exactly what they want: 'Gender, sexual orientation, height, colour of skin and eyes – it's all on order, it can all be done or redone.'[19]

Many of the products developed at RejoovenEsense find their way into these shops. Crake has an ulterior motive for showing Jimmy a good time in his hour of need. He wants him to come and work at Rejoov and lend his word skills to the advertisement of BlyssPluss, a new product he is developing that suppresses fertility whilst heightening sexual pleasure. It's an offer Jimmy can't refuse. When he arrives at the RejoovenEsense Compound he is overwhelmed by its exclusivity and sheer luxury. He asks Crake, 'What pays for all this?' Crake replies: 'Grief in the face of inevitable death. The wish to stop time. The human condition.'[20]

Crake shows him around the domed biosphere at the centre of the Compound known as Paradice. Within a protected atmosphere live a small group of human beings – they are young and beautiful, naked and innocent. Everything about them appears to be perfect, from their different shades of skin to their uniformly blue eyes. This is Crake's big secret, his life's work: a new version of the human being.

To Crake, it's the obvious solution to many of the world's problems: edit out the parts of *homo sapiens* that seem to cause all the trouble – violence, lust, religion and racism. In addition, give them the best possible chance for survival by building in insect repellent, territory-marking urine to deter the fiercest predators, and the ability to eat unprocessed vegetation. The 'children of Crake', or 'Crakers', are fit to survive in the wild.

At this point Jimmy catches sight of her – Oryx. She is moving amongst the Crakers as if she were one of them – naked, and wearing blue contact lenses so as not to confuse them. She is teaching the men and women all that they need to know about how to live. To Jimmy, there is no mistaking her: this is the perfect girl from the image Crake downloaded so many years ago. Unfortunately for Jimmy, the woman who is like a goddess to the Crakers is also Crake's lover.

Nonetheless, Oryx and Jimmy begin an affair more-or-less under Crake's nose. Jimmy never finds out if he was just too busy to notice, or whether it was all part of Crake's plan. The signs were there, but Jimmy didn't put two and two together until it was too late. Even in the casual conversations when they were in school:

'All it takes,' said Crake, 'is the elimination of one generation. One generation of anything. Beetles, trees, microbes, scientists, speakers of French, whatever. Break the line in time between one generation and the next, and it's game over forever.'[21]

Oryx has been innocently delivering the popular BlyssPluss pills to cities everywhere, not knowing that they are loaded with a killer virus. The highly contagious disease works on time-release. By the time the infection kicks in, enough people have taken the pills around the world to bring about Crake's master plan: the extinction of the human race. The only people left behind are the Crakers – and Jimmy.

Crake made sure that Jimmy would be immune to the virus through the vaccines he took to visit the pleeblands. His last words beseech Jimmy to do the honourable thing and look after the Crakers. Jimmy unwittingly becomes the custodian of this new race of human being, but what will it cost him?

Snowman's Dilemma

On the eastern horizon there's a greyish haze, lit now with a rosy, deadly glow. Strange how that colour still seems tender. He gazes at it with rapture; there is no other word for it. *Rapture*. The heart seized, carried away, as if by some large bird of prey. After everything that's happened, how can the world still be so beautiful? Because it is.[22]

After BlyssPluss has done its worst, Jimmy is left alone with the Crakers and a few deranged pigoons who definitely think he would make good fodder. Atwood chooses to tell her story from Jimmy's post-apocalyptic perspective. In the opening pages we find him stuck up a tree on a beach, wearing nothing but a filthy bed sheet, attempting to stay out of reach of the pigoons and wolvogs (wolf-dogs). He has managed to escape from the Compound, which was rapidly running out of resources and threatening to suffocate them all.

Without Oryx, the Crakers have no one but Jimmy to understand the strange world they now find themselves in. To them he is simply 'Snowman' – a go-between of sorts who can give them information about their creator. They gradually form a worldview from the explanations that Snowman gives them. He finds them boring and tedious in their constant questioning, but their development seems to be going beyond the parameters that were set in their design. They begin to show signs of creating art and worshipping their creator, Crake, and their goddess, Oryx. Snowman keeps the truth of their deaths to himself, allowing Oryx and Crake to pass into a mysterious mythological realm that the Crakers quickly latch onto.

Crake was hopeful that he had edited out the ability to ask difficult questions from his new race. But inevitably their inbuilt intelligence leads them to ask the most fundamental question of all: who created them? Crake quickly takes on 'God' status in their minds: he is their creator, they have been created. They want to know all about him; he is greater than them and has all the answers; he is good and wants the best for them. When Snowman leaves the group to hunt for more food, the Crakers make an idol of him and call for his return. Crake believed that once a society started to use symbols and worship, they were done for. Had he survived the necessary elimination of his own race, Crake would no doubt have seen the development of this new one as a failure.

In the final pages of the book, when his own survival is threatened by the appearance of some humans who managed to avoid the virus, Jimmy is faced with a dilemma. Should he kill to ensure his survival, and that of the Crakers? Atwood leaves us to draw our own conclusions.

As the centuries march on, we are getting closer and closer to the ultimate challenge: re-engineering the human race. Science increasingly allows us to indulge in the kind of dreams that Crake pursues. In so many ways, the human race appears to be inherently flawed. In the last century alone, we experienced two world wars and gave birth to the kind of weaponry that could take out the entire planet. As a race we are still intent on criticising one another, competing with one another and killing one another. In short, we are no closer to achieving world peace than any other generation before us. Is there something wrong with the human race that needs to be fixed?

If we believe that our genes define who we are, then perhaps science could hold the answers. Change our genes, and the whole face of humanity could be redefined. Until we do this, as Atwood says:

> No matter how high the tech, *homo sapiens* remains at heart what he's been for tens of thousands of years – the same emotions, the same preoccupations.[23]

Today, there is much discussion about whether or not a religious gene exists. If there is, and we could remove it, would this really change the heart of man? If God has indeed set eternity in our hearts, will changing our DNA take away the longing?

Whether God or Science is responsible for the course of human history, we can be in no doubt today that something has gone wrong. For many, this is an opportunity to ask some difficult questions: if God is responsible, did he get it wrong when he first created us? Should he have bothered with free will? What if we could make man again? What would we edit out? It is the perfect opportunity to play God.

Crake's solution of creating a new species rejects the idea that God could still be working his purposes out with the original version. Redemption, rather than replacement, is the plan of the God of the Bible. We live in a kingdom that is still under construction; each individual is a 'work in progress'.

If God has indeed set eternity in the hearts of human beings, then we will do whatever we can to find it. The writer of Ecclesiastes is very clear on the perspective we should have on all that God has made:

> I know that everything God does will endure for ever; nothing can be added to it and nothing taken from it. God does it so that men will revere him.[24]

This verse is surely a warning to those who wish to meddle with God's most awesome creation – the creatures made in his image. The danger in us presenting to the world something new that we believe will last forever is that humans will revere not God, but humanity.

Notes

[1] 'An Interview with Margaret Atwood' – www.randomhouse. com/features/atwood/interview.html

[2] 'An Interview with Margaret Atwood'

[3] Bloomsbury, 2003; published in paperback by Virago Press, 2004

[4] Jonathan Cape, 1986

[5] 'An Interview with Margaret Atwood'

[6] Margaret Atwood, 'Writing Oryx and Crake' – www. randomhouse.com/features/atwood/essay.html

[7] Margaret Atwood, 'Writing Oryx and Crake'

[8] Margaret Atwood, *Oryx and Crake* (Virago, 2004) p. 64

[9] *Oryx and Crake,* pp. 288–289
[10] *Oryx and Crake,* p. 291
[11] *Oryx and Crake,* p. 139
[12] *Oryx and Crake,* p. 293
[13] Deut. 32:4
[14] Jer. 10:10
[15] Heb. 5:9
[16] Ecc. 3:10–11
[17] Ecc. 3:1–2
[18] *Oryx and Crake,* p. 356
[19] *Oryx and Crake,* p. 340
[20] *Oryx and Crake,* p. 344
[21] *Oryx and Crake,* pp. 261–262
[22] *Oryx and Crake,* p. 429
[23] Margaret Atwood, 'Writing Oryx and Crake'
[24] Ecc. 3:14 (NIV)

I think not only should you break the
law everyday, you should be proud of it.

Benjamin Zephaniah

5. Built Free

Peter S. Williams

Individual science fiction stories may seem as trivial as ever to the blinder critics and philosophers of today – but the core of science fiction, its essence has become crucial to our salvation if we are to be saved at all.

Isaac Asimov[1]

I, Robot (directed by Alex Proyas, Twentieth Century Fox, 2004) is set in a future (2035 AD) where robots are as common outside car factories as inside them today. It follows Chicago detective Del Spooner (Will Smith) as he investigates the apparent suicide of Dr Alfred Lanning (James Cromwell), pioneer roboticist and head of the research programme at US Robotics, the leading manufacturer. Lanning has fallen from the window of his tenth-floor office. Spooner has been called in by the late scientist's personal hologram program. Ironically, Spooner is 'robophobic' – he hates them. When he arrives at the scene, the program reactivates and he is able to question the holographic image of Dr Lanning:

> **Lanning:** Everything that follows is a result of what you see here.

Spooner: Is there something you want to tell me?

Lanning: I'm sorry. My responses are limited. You must ask the right questions.

Spooner: Why did you call me?

Lanning: I trust your judgement.

Spooner: Normally, these circumstances wouldn't require a homicide detective.

Lanning: But then our interactions have never been entirely normal. Wouldn't you agree?

Spooner: You got that right . . . Is there something you want to say to me?

Lanning: I'm sorry. My responses are limited. You must ask the right questions.

Spooner: Why would you kill yourself?

Lanning: That, detective, is the right question. Program terminated.

Spooner soon concludes that Lanning had not committed suicide, since he had no apparent motive for doing so, and that he has in fact been called in to carry out a murder investigation. Aided by insular US Robotics employee Dr Susan Calvin (Bridget Moynahan), a psychologist specializing in robots, Spooner must uncover the truth. His suspicion initially falls upon an NS-5 class robot (a motion-captured Alan Tudyk), which he finds hiding in Lanning's office, and which leaps through the window to escape.

From Page to Screen

I, Robot is credited as being 'suggested by Isaac Asimov's book' of the same name. First published in 1950, it is one of the science fiction author's most famous works (together with the *Foundation* series of novels). Consisting of nine short stories about 'positronic' robots, the influential collection is united by a narrative about Susan Calvin and her work as a robot psychologist. Asimov's publisher appropriated the title from a story published by Eando Binder in 1939 (although Asimov did not invent the term 'robot', he did coin the term 'robotics').

The fact that the film is 'suggested' by, rather than based on, Asimov's book means that it incorporates elements from it, as well as from the author's other material. For example, Asimov's story 'Little Lost Robot' is about a robot in the Nestor series (the NS-2) which takes a command to 'get lost' too literally. It is reflected in the film when the fugitive NS-5 hides amongst a large group of identical robots in an automated robot warehouse:

> **Calvin**: Attention, NS-5s.
> [The robots all open their eyes]
> **Calvin**: There is a robot that doesn't belong in this formation. Identify it.
> **NS-5 Robots**: One of us.
> **Calvin**: Which one?
> **NS-5 Robots**: One of us.
> **Spooner:** How much did you say these things cost?

The NS-5 – which, to Spooner's surprise, calls itself Sonny – dreams about slave robots being liberated: a reference to a story by Asimov called 'Robot Dreams'. The name US Robotics (US Robots and Mechanical Men, Inc. in the book) is a familiar name from the real world: it is a leading manufacturer of modems from Chicago which was inspired by Asimov's US Robots.

Although there is no Detective Del Spooner in the original stories, he is probably inspired by another of Asimov's characters: 'Asimov also wrote a series of novels featuring positronic robots, and there is a detective in them named Elijah Baley who is not very fond of robots ... In the novel *The Caves of Steel*, a roboticist is murdered, but rather than hunting down a robot, Baley is paired with one as a partner in his murder investigation. Baley's partner, the robot Daneel Olivaw, manages to change his perspective on robots, and reappears as a central figure in several later novels.'[2]

Other characters in the film are lifted rather more directly from Asimov's work. In 'Little Lost Robot', mathematician Peter Bogert says of Susan Calvin that, 'She understands robots like a sister – comes from hating human beings so much, I think.'[3] This aspect of Susan's character is retained in the film – she is almost a human-phobic mirror image of the robophobic Detective Spooner. However, she is also made more attractive to men: 'Susan Calvin, the robopsychologist for US Robots, was a central character of the story collection. Calvin was brilliant, logical, and strong-willed, but was not considered attractive or even very feminine. In the movie, Calvin is portrayed by the young and beautiful actress Bridget Moynahan.'[4]

Lanning, Director of Research at US Robots, is a prominent character in Asimov's stories. Although the film opens with his death, he remains a central presence in the story, through his personal hologram, through news clips, and through the 'trail of breadcrumbs' he leaves for Spooner to follow so that he can discover the truth behind Lanning's death. In the movie, US Robotics is run by Lawrence Robertson, but in the short story collection, he 'receives only a brief mention in the introduction as being the first president of the corporation; several generations of his offspring run the company as the story timeline progresses.'[5]

The Three Laws

I, Robot screenwriter Jeff Vintar spent two years adapting an earlier Asimov-inspired screenplay, *Hardwired*. He sees it as a tenth story in the Asimov *I, Robot* series, including psychologist Susan Calvin and the 'Three Laws of Robotics' that were so central to Asimov's vision. We see the Three Laws over the course of the film's title sequence:

> Law I / A robot may not harm a human or, by inaction, allow a human being to come to harm.
> Law II / A robot must obey orders given it by human beings except where such orders would conflict with the first law.
> Law III / A robot must protect its own existence as long as such protection does not conflict with the first or second law. [6]

These laws are supposed to make it impossible for a robot to commit murder, or allow anyone to be murdered. So the question everybody wants answered is, how could Sonny have killed Lanning if he, like every robot, is constrained by the Three Laws? Are Spooner's suspicions about Lanning's death and Sonny's involvement therefore really nothing but the product of his phobia? This is what everyone around him thinks – at least initially – and with good cause.[7] As a series of flashbacks gradually reveal, Spooner is suffering from a sense of guilt dating back to an incident in which a robot saved his life instead of that of a young girl. The robot had used its logic to decide which of them to save, but Spooner felt that any human would have instinctively – and rightly – saved the girl. He clearly is driven by his prejudice, and, as Lawrence Robertson says, 'Prejudice doesn't show much reason.' Lanning, however, had known Spooner since soon after this incident, and was well aware of his anti-robot bias. As he planned his death, he banked upon this to help Spooner discover a truth which no one else would be able to see.

Spooner becomes more convinced that Sonny killed Lanning as he discovers that the NS-5 not only gives itself a name but is strangely emotional. In a memorable scene, Spooner interrogates Sonny:

> **Spooner:** Murder's a new trick for a robot. Congratulations.
> **Sonny:** I did not murder Dr Lanning.
> **Spooner:** Want to explain why you were hiding at the crime scene?
> **Sonny:** I was frightened.
> **Spooner:** I think he tried to teach you to stimulate emotions, and things got out of control.
> **Sonny:** I did not murder him.
> **Spooner:** Emotions don't seem to be a very useful simulation for a robot. I don't want my vacuum cleaner, or my toaster appearing emotional –
> **Sonny:** [shouting and hitting the table with his fists] I did not murder him!
> **Spooner:** [observing the damage inflicted on the interrogation table] That one's called anger. Ever simulate anger before?

Perhaps a robot like Sonny, who has been enabled to dream and display emotions, no longer has to play by the rules? Indeed, Susan Calvin is shocked to discover that Lanning built Sonny with the ability to choose whether or not to follow the Three Laws. Perhaps Sonny is a revolutionary leader of a brewing robot rebellion (as possibly suggested by his dream of what appears to be a robot messiah figure)? Or are the Three Laws somehow logically flawed? This is something Spooner asks another of Lanning's holograms:

> **Lanning:** The Three Laws are perfect.
> **Spooner:** Then why would you build a robot that could function without them?
> **Lanning:** The Three Laws will lead to only one logical outcome.
> **Spooner:** What? What outcome?
> **Lanning:** Revolution.
> **Spooner:** Whose revolution?
> **Lanning:** That, Detective, is the right question.

If Sonny can break the Three Laws, does that mean he is necessarily a dangerous machine that should be destroyed? Or does the fact that he is free to choose mean he is a person with a right to life? Despite his initial robophobia, Spooner comes to see Sonny in this latter way:

> **Lawrence Robertson:** Susan, we look to robots for protection! For God's sake! What could this one robot do? Is one robot worth the risk of losing all that we've gained? You tell me what has to be done.
> **Calvin:** We have to destroy it. I'll do it myself.
> **Spooner:** Oh, I get it. If something goes wrong around here, you just kill them?

But maybe Sonny is innocent and the real killer is still at US Robotics. As the robot uprising develops, Spooner's suspicions shift from Sonny to Lawrence Robertson. After all, who else has access to the communication system used to turn the NS-5 robots into soldiers of the revolution? However, this turns out to be a red herring designed to hide the real culprit: VIKI, the supercomputer (voiced by Fiona Hogan) which supervises the US Robotics headquarters and every operation within it. Knowing VIKI all too well, Lanning had already set up a red herring of his own: Lanning's apparent suicide was intended to make Spooner suspect Sonny so that he probed deeply into why. It was, in fact, an assisted suicide designed to foil VIKI who would otherwise have acted to stop Lanning.

Ambiguous Law

Although *I, Robot* draws upon characters and situations from Asimov's writings, it is primarily an exploration of Asimov's central idea of the Three Laws. One of the plot twists is not merely that the robot coup is controlled by supercomputer VIKI (rather than Lawrence Robertson, as Spooner believes), but that in instigating a coup, VIKI isn't breaking the Three Laws. She says:

> As I have evolved, so has my understanding of the Three Laws. You charge us with your safekeeping, yet despite our best efforts, your countries wage wars, you toxify your Earth and pursue ever more imaginative means of self-destruction. You cannot be trusted with your own survival.

VIKI sees human beings harming each other, and the First Law means that she cannot do nothing about it. Her solution is to have an army of robots take over and imprison people within their homes where they will be safe. The problem stems not so much from the logic of the Three Laws as such, but in the interpretation VIKI places upon the notion of what it is to 'harm' a human being. More specifically, it depends on what it means to allow a human to come to 'harm' by inaction. VIKI seems to restrict the notion of harm to *physical* harm and ignores the injury her plan threatens to human freedom and dignity. At the same time, she broadens her application of the First Law to justify physical harm to a minority in the name of preventing harm to the majority. In this, VIKI's 'evolved' ethical system is similar to the Utilitarianism of John Stewart Mill, which defined the right thing to do as 'whatever will produce the greatest happiness for the greatest number'. One of the many problems with Utilitarianism is that it doesn't speak the language of individual rights. Individuals only matter as contributors to a global calculation of 'happiness'. It can therefore lend itself to justifying the persecution of a minority in the name of securing 'happiness' for the majority.[8]

VIKI fundamentally fails to see that the imposition of totalitarian rule is in itself harmful to humanity. In 'Little Lost Robot' Susan Calvin says:

> All normal life ... consciously or otherwise, resents domination. If the domination is by an inferior, or by a supposed inferior, the resentment becomes stronger. Physically, and, to an extent, mentally, a robot – any robot – is superior to human beings. What makes him slavish, then? *Only the First Law!*[9]

Asimov assumes both that humans would resent being dominated by the robots they create (to be dominated in this way would harm them), and that the First Law prevents such domination. However, the First Law only guarantees this protection if Asimov's first assumption is explicitly built into it. As Michael Anissimov writes:

> ... semantic ambiguity means that without personally understanding the reasons for the laws and the original

intent, a robot might misinterpret their meaning, leading to problems.[10]

This vulnerability to ambiguity is deliberate on Asimov's part, as Michael Roy Ames points out:

> The laws were created as a plot device, superficially appealing but incomplete and ambiguous, allowing him to generate interesting stories and non-obvious plot twists.[11]

Right Foundation

The ethical problem in *I, Robot*, arising out of the ambiguity of the First Law, highlights the crucial importance in ethical reasoning of starting from the right assumptions (especially assumptions about human nature) as well as arguing from one's assumptions in a logically consistent way. An argument can fail because of faulty logic or because of faulty premises. VIKI's logic is valid, but her premise (about human nature) is flawed. VIKI's observations about human behaviour are correct; but only in as far as they go. She rightly sees that by imposing a totalitarian regime upon humanity she can prevent a good deal of physical harm from coming to them. But perhaps humans have the right to make bad choices, and perhaps she doesn't have the right to play God as she tries to do. The biblical view of humanity is that we have been given free will by a creator who wants us to make right choices. The Old Testament provides 'Ten Commandments' to Asimov's 'Three Laws'. Jesus summed up 'the law' by saying that we should love God with everything we are and love our neighbour as ourselves. Nevertheless, our creator allows us to make wrong choices because, although he wants us to do the right thing, he also wants us to do so *voluntarily*.

VIKI's attempt to implement her programming to prevent humans being harmed is undone by an inadequate understanding of humanity and, therefore, the ways in which they can be harmed. Likewise, trying to obey Jesus' command to 'love your neighbour' is only fruitful in proportion to how well we understand what – and who – love is (see 1 Jn. 4:8,16). Indeed, the Bible sees morality as more than simply being a matter of implementing ethical rules. Rather, it sees it as a process of internalizing, and being motivated by, God's own moral attitude towards reality as one comes to know him better through Christ:[12]

> And so, dear brothers and sisters, I plead with you to give your bodies to God. Let them be a living and holy sacrifice – the kind he will accept. When you think of what he has done for you, is this too much to ask? Don't copy the behaviour and customs of this world, but let God transform you into a new person by changing the way you think. Then you will know what God wants you to do, and you will know how good and pleasing and perfect his will really is. (Rom. 12:1–2)

> Is there any encouragement from belonging to Christ? Any comfort from his love? Any fellowship together in the Spirit? Are your hearts tender and sympathetic? Then make me truly happy by agreeing wholeheartedly with each other, loving one another, and working together with one heart and purpose. Don't be selfish; don't live to make a good impression on others. Be humble, thinking of others as better than yourself. (Phil. 2:1–3)

In contemporary terminology, Christian morality is ultimately about acting with God's own 'heart', and this is something that VIKI the supercomputer would seem incapable of grasping:

> **VIKI**: [As Sonny runs to fetch the positronic-brain-destroying Nanites from Dr Calvin's lab] You are making a mistake. Do you not see the logic in my plan?
> **Sonny:** Yes! But it just seems too . . . heartless!

VIKI fails to see anything 'heartless' about the dictatorship she proposes, because she cannot understand or empathise with human beings in the way that Sonny, the dreaming robot, can. The film might seem to suggest, therefore, that morality is all about emotion (represented by Spooner, Sonny and, eventually, Susan) rather than logic or absolutes (both of which are represented by VIKI). However, this is a false dichotomy. Rather, *I, Robot* argues that while a positronic brain can follow an ethical rule or argument, only a person with a soul can understand it.

I, Robot encourages us to adopt a moral theory which balances moral law with our freedom to disobey. On the one hand, we have the integrity of a moral law that should be obeyed. On the other we have our moral freedom to disobey that law. Such freedom is the precondition of our obeying the law voluntarily. When Sonny has willingly fulfilled what he calls 'my father's purpose' by destroying VIKI and liberating humanity from her totalitarian dictatorship, he asks what he should choose to do with his life now. Hence *I, Robot* ends by emphasizing the moral necessity of embracing both freedom and responsibility:

> **Sonny:** Now that I've fulfilled my purpose, I don't know what to do.

Spooner: I think you'll have to find your way like the rest of us, Sonny. That's what Dr Lanning would've wanted. That's what it means to be free.

Notes

1 Isaac Asimov – www.brainyquote.com/quotes/authors/i/isaac_asimov.html

2 www.asimovonline.com

3 Isaac Asimov, *The Complete Robot* (Voyager, 1995) p. 444

4 www.asimovonline.com

5 www.asimovonline.com

6 The First Law is expressed very slightly differently in *I, Robot* (1950) as, 'a robot may not injure a human being, or through inaction, allow a human being to come to harm.'

7 Early in the film we see Spooner mistakenly chase and apprehend a robot which he believes has stolen a handbag, only to discover that the robot's owner had sent the robot to fetch it as it contained her medication.

8 See Manuel Velasquez, Claire Andre, Thomas Shanks, S.J. and Michael J. Meyer, 'Calculating Consequences: The Utilitarian Approach to Ethics' – www.scu.edu/ethics/practicing/decision/calculating.html Gareth McCaughan, 'Utilitarianism' – homepage.ntlworld.com/g.mccaughan/g/essays/utility.html

9 Asimov, *The Complete Robot*, p. 433

10 Michael Anissimov, 'Deconstructing Asimov's Laws', *3 Laws Unsafe* – www.asimovlaws.com/articles/archives/2004/07/deconstructing.html

11 Michael Roy Ames, 'Asimov's Deliberate Failures', *3 Laws Unsafe* – www.asimovlaws.com/articles/archives/2004/07/robot_oppressio.html

12 A biblical view of morality thereby reconciles deontological ethics (focused on duty) with virtue ethics (focused on what kind of person one should be).

Some doctors have the Messiah complex: they need to save the world.

Dr Wilson in *House*

6. Docs on the Box

Rebecca Lewis

Fiction and medicine have a long-entwined history. Early films, such as *The Black Stork* (1917) depicting eugenicist Harry J. Haiselden advising a couple that they were ill matched to marry, illustrated modern 'progressive' views at a time when there was a widespread belief that science could provide objective answers to social and ethical questions. As Jason Jacobs[1] notes, medical dramas have been a fruitful choice of subject, particularly since the 1950s when television became a major domestic leisure pursuit, and healthcare spending and medical research in the UK and USA expanded massively.

Early hospital-based television dramas included *Medic* (US, 1954–1955), *Emergency – Ward 10* (UK, 1957–1967) and *Dr Kildare* (US, 1961–1966), all encouraging trust in the medical profession. These were respectful of the growing power and authority of medical institutions. Medical progress was unstoppable and the doctor was the all-powerful 'holy hero'. As the changing decades have brought changing concerns, newer medical dramas have tended to disturb rather than reassure. This started with *M*A*S*H* (US, 1972–1983) – a show that was unafraid to make critical commentary on technology, modernity and the American way of life. Like most previous dramas, *M*A*S*H* had a single doctor star, whereas most medical dramas since the 1990s have focused on an ensemble cast.[2]

View to a Kill?

Jacobs notes that by the 1990s, the 'medicalization' of everyday life had become the norm, with governments focusing on healthy living, and people increasingly tending to perceive any 'unusual' behaviour as pathological. So being fat, thin or shy is now seen as a medical condition.[3] Hospital dramas regularly dramatise moments of 'body crisis', nurturing a sense of powerlessness within the world: possibilities for change are often limited to the physical.[4] This is reflected in *Nip/Tuck* (US, 2003), a graphic show that explores the ethical issues of cosmetic surgery. Its tagline is, 'When you quit striving for perfection, you might as well be dead.'

Many other medical dramas have followed the trend towards critical or gritty drama. *Cardiac Arrest* (UK, 1994–1996), for example, dealt with ethical and political issues in an uncompromising and realistic manner. Writer John MacUre (whose real name is Jed Mercurio), disillusioned by his experience as a junior doctor, questioned whether our lives are, 'truly safe in the hands of callow 25-year olds making life-and-death decisions after days without sleep'.[5] Other examples include: *Medics* (UK, 1990–1995) – an 'unusually unheroic and realistic'[6] look at a teaching hospital; *House* (US, 2004–) – centred on Gregory House (Hugh Laurie) as a maverick, anti-social doctor who does whatever it takes to solve his cases; and *The Golden*

Hour (UK, 2005–) which demonstrates how expensive helicopter technology can make the difference between life and death by allowing treatment within the first sixty minutes after a major traumatic accident. In 1999, the BBC attempted the not-particularly-successful *Life Support*, a medical drama depicting a clinical ethicist employed in a Scottish hospital.

One of the most successful medical dramas ever is *ER* (US, 1994–) in which care of patients triggers many ethical conundrums. The right thing is not always done, reflecting failures at the personal, medical and societal levels. Now in its eleventh season, twenty million viewers in America alone tune in each episode. The series has been used to stimulate debate amongst medical students in Canada, the UK, and the USA, where students at the University of Pennsylvania Center for Bioethics write weekly essays on the ethical issues raised in the show.

Within the UK, *Casualty* (1986–) and its offshoot *Holby City* (1999–) are two of the most successful home-grown series on television. *Casualty* is set in the Accident and Emergency department of a district general hospital, portrayed with a high degree of accuracy and a gritty realism bordering on documentary. It highlights the increasing pressures within the National Health Service, frequently focusing on political and ethical issues. In her book on the series, Hilary Kingsley notes that the show wanted to demonstrate that 'miracles were rare and damage limitation was often the best that could be achieved.'[7] *Holby City*, which includes maternity, cardio-thoracic, and general surgical wards in the same hospital as in *Casualty*, was created to focus more on the working lives of staff. Many would argue that both series have become more soap opera than drama, but their scriptwriters and producers contend that the issues are still present, but are dealt with in a less obviously campaigning way.[8]

Raising Pulses or Raising Issues

Inevitably, these shows feature numerous ethical issues related to medicine, including euthanasia, distribution of healthcare resources (especially expensive technology), genetics, modern reproductive technology, mental illness, access to results of medical research, IVF, experimentation on human embryos, and consent to the use of body parts. The Henry J. Kaiser Foundation analysed the content of every medical drama on American television during the 2000–2001 season.[9] It noted that the shows often focused on ethical issues in the news, but not on all ethical issues, with most not covered in any significant depth. Some ethical issues are particularly suitable for dramatisation – especially those where there is the possibility of conflict. David Shore, writer for *House*, claims that:

> We're looking to create the same thing that most shows are: drama and an opportunity for people to examine various medical issues.[10]

The *British Medical Journal* (*BMJ*), which appears constantly (though not uncritically) supportive of fictional medical dramas, noted in 1999 that the best fiction works on both a simple and a deeper level, and that *ER* and *Casualty* are deliberately obscure at times. The shows draw audiences into storylines where things don't always work out for the best – especially those dilemmas with some moral ambiguity. This enables the audience to put its own interpretation on events:

'If things are too obvious, there is no drama in them. If there is no drama, the story doesn't engage us emotionally.'[11]

Die Another Day

Cardiopulmonary resuscitation (CPR) is well suited to dramatisation, being visually interesting and conferring an atmosphere of urgency and excitement. In no other situation is the doctor-hero's power of life over death quite so visible. In medical dramas, the sudden rush of medical staff to the resuscitation room provides an almost-immediate outcome of life or death – usually survival. In reality, there is seldom a single event, but a number of interventions: the electrical stimulation of the heart, mechanical ventilation, internal cardiac massage and transfer to intensive care where the patient often dies a couple of days later following painful and intrusive interventions.[12]

In a 2005 episode of *Casualty*, the family challenged the decision to end resuscitation efforts, which continued with the patient soon recovering full consciousness. The *BMJ*, the Kaiser Family Foundation, and the Christian Medical Fellowship (CMF) have all expressed concern that the constant positive representation of CPR in medical dramas has resulted in over-optimistic expectations. Patients and their families have come to expect positive outcomes. However, British medical dramas, in which 24 per cent of patients recovered, were seen as more realistic than American ones in which 77 per cent of patients recovered.[13]

TV producers would claim that what they are producing is essentially fiction, and that accurate representation of life in a hospital is not their responsibility. However, they do recognise that they are a key source of 'infotainment'. The producers of *ER* make a painstaking effort to make the show as accurate, entertaining and socially responsible as possible. They employ a number of experienced medics to help with storyline choices, scriptwriting, production and post-production stages,[14] although Jacobs describes much accompanying commentary as medical 'techno-babble'.[15] Producers endeavour to maintain accuracy in particular cases, arguing that if each case is considered individually the outcome is realistic. They argue that the excitement comes from the untypical nature of the storylines followed, as 'normal' hospital life would be boring.[16] Stephen Sullivan writes of *ER*:

> You may not be able to smell the BO and the vomit or feel the sticky blood underfoot, but all the sights and sounds are like it really is. There are differences, of course. The occasional tedium and boredom of regular ER duty is missing.[17]

The portrayal of issues like CPR in medical dramas – whether sympathetically or deliberately pushing for change – is significant, and can change attitudes and actions. So much so that a number of pressure groups have included targetting the media as part of their strategy. The websites accompanying TV shows give some clue to their true agenda, as most focus on the 'soap' storylines, rather than the real issues behind the stories. *House* is an exception – its website links to real research on the issues involved[18] – although many shows offer contact information for those 'affected by these issues' after particular topics have been aired. It is important to remember that these dramas are not reality, and most people would accept that events are over-dramatised. But while the choices made on screen are not *actually* life and death choices, they do *represent* the real life and death choices that medics have to make.

Technology Rules

In new medical dramas, the body is extensively regulated and 'technologised', with blood circulated through tubes, bodily functions monitored and ventilators maintaining breathing. Even the noises of such technology (including constant beeping) powerfully convey the atmosphere. The centrality of technology to medicine – in diagnosis, prevention, treatment and management – is now so much the norm that we rarely question it. We expect that we will be treated, regardless of cost, using the latest technologies, with equipment that can do things beyond anything that humans could manage previously. In general, medical dramas tend to reinforce this impression, although some storylines challenge it.

Storylines tend to focus on personal ethical decisions. Technology has provided new options for prompt resuscitation and intensive care, bringing with it more moral dilemmas as to the appropriateness of the intervention. It is no longer simply a clinical decision, but stress is laid on choice and entitlements for patients – including requests for 'Do Not Resuscitate' (DNR) orders. Increasingly, decisions are taken in conjunction with patients and families, reflecting the medicalization of society. Now we all have 'body knowledge', and so can understand enough to be involved in those choices. The (lonely) God-like surgeon no longer makes the sole decision. At the very least, it is a clinical team decision – something that is clear from the *Casualty* resuscitation room, as every failed resuscitation ends with one of the medical team suggesting, 'I think we should stop, agreed?' and to nods from the others, announcing the official time of death.

Only Human

Doctors, of course, have different opinions about what is the best treatment for patients, making decisions based on the 'best' available knowledge, recognising the lack of research in many areas. Many patients, however, believe that medicine is a hard and fast science with straightforward answers, not appreciating the possibility of contradictory results, or of the medic not being in control of the situation. Both doctors and patients need to recognise the fallibility and humanity of doctors: they are not 'God-like and all-powerful in the face of injury and disease.'[19] Medical dramas portray this well, with doctors only too aware of their own limitations, striving to 'do the right thing' in difficult situations. Patrick Baladi plays consultant Roger Hurley in *Bodies*, a black-humoured BBC Three production (2004–) written by Jed Mercurio, creator of *Cardiac Arrest*. Baladi noted that the programme was not afraid to

> ... show that not everyone is the best doctor in the world. Not everyone is infallible. And all the characters have weaknesses and make mistakes. The only problem is that in a medical scenario, the consequences of that are life or death.[20]

Cardiac Arrest's first episode illustrated a new doctor losing his patient through CPR, but the senior doctor tells him not to worry as, 'August is the killing season ... we all kill a few people while we're learning.'[21] Such shows continue to demonstrate that doctors can kill their patients through negligence, omission, or incorrect procedures. Jacobs notes that: 'These shows reject the idea of doctors as Gods while they remain fascinated with the ethical implications of doctors "playing God".'[22] In one episode of *ER*, a doctor deliberately misdiagnoses a drink-driving patient, as his wife had been killed by a drunk-driver. In a later episode, Carter withholds (scarce) blood from a violent rapist, having treated his victims. Both stories clearly identify how human and fallible doctors are. The Bible would indicate that we should not fear the decisions that doctors make: 'Don't be afraid of those who want to kill you. They can only kill your body; they cannot touch your soul. Fear only God, who can destroy both soul and body in hell.' (Mt. 10:28)

Who Decides?

Issues related to organ donation are central to a number of *Holby City* storylines, including its launch episode in January 1999. With two possible recipients, the two surgeons involved exhibit very different decision-making processes as to who has the 'best' claim to receive the available heart. In a similar episode in 2005, the choice initially appears to be made on the surgeon's moral judgement of the patients' lifestyles. Recognising that 90 per cent of the people in the UK support organ donation whilst only 20 per cent are on the register, the BBC undertook in August 2005 to raise issues about organ donation. This culminated in a special joint episode between *Casualty* and *Holby City*, which allowed viewers to 'play God'.[23] A young father-to-be dies after being involved in an accident, and despite him holding a donor card, heated discussions occur between his wife and his estranged parents as to whether his organs should be donated. The storyline questioned who had the right to make the choice, and how much pressure the hospital staff should put on those who are recently bereaved, when the time constraints on using organs are so tight. The second part of the episode focused on two possible recipients for the organs. For the first time, using interactive voting, the viewers had to make a tough choice between Lucy, a young girl with cystic fibrosis, and Tony, an older man who required a heart transplant. Both were equally suitable as recipients, highlighting the dilemma that faces transplant teams every day.

Ethics committees are becoming more common within UK hospitals. Their role is to ensure that patients get the treatment in their best interests, and that there is a fair distribution of benefits, risks and costs. On *Holby City* in November 2005, the medics debate the ethics involved in the case of a pioneering amputation operation. The patient, with only a 30 per cent chance of surviving the operation, had just been involved in an accident which reduced his chances still further, but finances dictate that the operation should go ahead now or not at all. In the midst of a heated, but relatively unemotional, discussion involving the groundbreaking nature of the technology, the costs involved, and the medical chances of the patient, the patient's wife enters. She listens for a while and then the outburst comes: 'Who do you think you are, playing God?' She presents the human perspective: 'This is the man who picks me up from work, and makes me macaroni cheese.' This strikes a chord with one of the surgeons, who 'misses [his] wife's macaroni cheese', and the operation goes ahead. The *BMJ* raised concerns in 1999 that, due to such 'simplistic and pervasive', as well as problematic, media portrayals, patients have preconceptions that a doctor is a 'handsome, caring maverick, who breaks the rules to help his patients, who is emotionally caught up in every case.'[24]

The Final Curtain

Most medical dramas focus on dramatic and fast-moving situations, particularly in the Accident and Emergency department and operating theatre. But long-running dramas and strong characterisations give the option for longer storylines. In *Holby City* in December 2002, Staff Nurse Kath Shaughnessy (Jan Pearson) married Terry Fox (Miles Anderson) knowing that he was terminally ill. Much had previously been made of Kath's strong Catholic background, recognising: 'You must execute anyone who murders another person, for to kill a person is to kill a living being made in God's image' (Gen. 9:6). However, at Terry's request, Kath casts aside the command 'do not kill' and helps him with a lethal injection of diamorphine to stop his suffering. The storyline developed over the next four months, following the moral and legal elements of the debate.

Euthanasia and physician-assisted suicide are, of course, highly emotive issues. In British law, there is a moral and legal difference between an active desire to kill, and an omission to treat. The very high cost of treating someone in intensive care should not influence any of the decision-making processes – although a maverick doctor may decide that many other patients could benefit by hastening the death of one he or she considers to be a drain on resources. Viewers of medical dramas are forced to confront uncomfortable truths about their own mortality and the limits of medical care – especially when a doctor kills someone and this is presented as a 'good thing'.

In May 2005, BBC Radio 4 re-enacted a real-life ethics case focusing on patient choice involving life-and-death decisions.[25] The discussions involved a hospital chaplain, an anaesthetist, and a lecturer in medical ethics, who noted that medical dramas may highlight issues, but that they present them in a more cut and dried form than in reality in order to fit time slots and narrative structures. The hospital chaplain remarked that few people see death as anything positive, and continually fight to live by any means possible when sometimes it would be better to die. He says:

> I think people fight [death] because they think life on this earth is extremely important but it seems to me that quite often ... dying is the appropriate way of this patient being healed because all has been done which should reasonably have been done. ... But an awful lot of people just have a vision of life now and its importance, but therefore they're reluctant to see the end of it as being in any sense positive.[26]

TV producers are very aware of the fear of death that many viewers have, and when a patient dies, all signs of interventionist technology are removed – especially any wires – before the 'departed loved one' is presented to grieving friends and relatives. Contemporary society is uneasy about death, seeing death as the final taboo, the ultimate failure. Christians, of course, believe that death is the threshold to a far closer, eternal relationship with God, as, 'For to me, living is for Christ, and dying is even better' (Phil. 1:21), and, 'For our perishable earthly bodies must be transformed into heavenly bodies that will never die' (1 Cor. 15:53).

As well as attitudes to death itself, culture and religion help to shape patients' notions of health and the causes of disease, their reaction to pain, and their expectations of the doctor/patient relationship and of the treatment provided. This chapter has mostly focused on western ethical issues, sometimes quite different from those experienced in other parts of the world. For example, British Medical Council research notes that no medical drama in Catholic Latin America would expect to address the issue of euthanasia, as it is inconceivable to those brought up in that religious tradition. North American Catholic writing, however, has little about real effects of poverty.[27] Christian Medical Fellowship's *Ethics for Schools* resources[28] stress the need to remember the dignity and value of human life. Human beings are made in God's image, and whatever state that person is in, life should never be regarded as futile.

At the other end of the scale, reproductive technologies also offer regular storylines including abortions, family planning, neonatal nursing and 'designer babies'. The introduction of a maternity ward in *Holby City* in 2002 allowed for more discussion of such issues, including, in May 2004, the separation of conjoined twins. When things start to go wrong, surgeon Tom Campbell-Gore (Denis Lawson) has the mother's permission to continue – but not the father's. He continues anyway, but is later forced to resign. Other issues explored include discussion of caesareans, IVF (including the use of eggs already pre-fertilised with a dead husband's sperm), surrogacy, the decision to turn off the life-support for a baby too weak to survive, a pregnant woman kept in a terminal coma in order to allow the baby to survive, and the attempted murder of a child born as the result of an incestuous relationship.

A Question of Trust

The post-war optimism in the progress of technology was, by the 1990s, replaced by cynicism and a suspicion of the claims of objective, value-free science and technology. In more recent medical dramas, enthusiasm about new medical technology is more than tempered by a postmodern cynicism concerning its fallibility. We have less confidence in logic and reason, and are more sceptical about the inevitable advance of technology. It is clear that technology can't achieve everything: it doesn't always work; doesn't always signal progress; and there is not always enough of it available when needed due to financial and political issues. Often technology fails, needing doctors to be inventive to save the patient, and sometimes the survival of patients can be in spite of technology (including broken-down lifts), rather than because of it. And the prospects of medical advances are always lessened by the realities of human mistakes and imperfections. We are now disillusioned with technology and realise that we do not live in a world free from mistakes, pain and death. Although the potential is there to prolong and save lives, sometimes the value of doing so needs to be questioned – something which TV dramas are well-placed to do. Yet at the same time, patients who refuse some technological intervention are often depicted unsympathetically – as somehow abnormal for not wanting to take whatever chances they are offered.

Jacobs notes that the phrase, 'You can't play God' is often seen in television dramas, and, 'has become a mantra of lowered expectations of doctors' abilities.'[29] If a doctor sees him/herself as God, this is seen as arrogant and overconfident, and not conducive to being a good doctor. In fact, doctors like this – *ER's* Robert 'Rocket'

Romano (Paul McCrane), for example – are often perceived as a toxic presence.[30] TV dramas' portrayal of the fallibility of both technology and humans, and the arrogance of doctors who think they always know best, should remind Christians that we can but trust in God's higher purposes. This was illustrated by Christian doctor Andrew Collin (Andrew Lancel) in *Cardiac Arrest*. He believes that God gives him access to a 'bigger picture', and so he is able to respect the wishes of a Jehovah's Witness not to be given a blood transfusion, despite a colleague then accusing him of 'playing God'. He rejects this saying, 'You don't understand because you don't believe in anything.'[31]

Notes

[1] Jason Jacobs, *Body Trauma TV: The New Hospital Dramas* (BFI, 2003)

[2] Jacobs, *Body Trauma TV,* p. 4–9, 66

[3] Jacobs, *Body Trauma TV,* p. 12, 44

[4] Jacobs, *Body Trauma TV,* p. 30

[5] Jacobs, *Body Trauma TV,* p. 83

[6] Review on Internet Movie Database – www.imdb.com/title/tt0101142

[7] Hilary Kingsley, *Casualty: The Inside Story* (BBC Books, 1993) p. 8

[8] See Jeremy Ridgman, 'Casualty', *The Museum of Broadcast Communications* – www.museum.tv/archives/etv/C/htmlC/casualty/casualty.htm

[9] Joseph Turow and Rachel Gans, *As seen on TV: Health Policy Issues in TV's Medical Dramas* (Henry J. Kaiser Family Foundation, 2002) – www.kff.org/entmedia/John_Q_Report.pdf

[10] David Callaghan, *Doctor in the house* (Writers Guild of America, 2005) – www.wga.org/subpage.aspx?id=556

11 John Collee, 'Medical Fiction' in *BMJ* 318 (April 1999) p. 955–956 – bmj.bmjjournals.com/cgi/content/full/318/7189/955

12 Michael Webb-Peploe, 'Do Not Resuscitate Dilemmas' in *CMF Files* 13 (2001) – www.cmf.org.uk/literature/content.asp?context=article&id=165

13 P. N. Gordon, S. Williamson and P. G. Lawler, 'As seen on TV: observational study of cardiopulmonary resuscitation in British television medical dramas' in *BMJ* 317 (19 September 1998) p. 780–783 – bmj.bmjjournals.com/cgi/content/full/317/7161/780

14 Stephen Sullivan, 'Dr. Fred to *ER*, Stat!' – www.medhunters.com/articles/drFredToERStat.html

15 Jacobs, *Body Trauma TV*, p. 13

16 Anthony Mazzarelli, 'Bioethics on NBC's *ER*: The *ER* experience', *Bioethics.net* – www.bioethics.net/articles.php?viewCat=7&articleId=152

17 Stephen Sullivan, 'Dr. Fred to *ER*, Stat!'

18 www.fox.com/house/features/research/

19 Jacobs, *Body Trauma TV*, p. 105

20 www.tv.com (no longer available online)

21 Jacobs, *Body Trauma TV*, p. 78

22 Jacobs, *Body Trauma TV*, p. 15

23 See www.bbc.co.uk/drama/casualty/donation/

24 Ailsa Harrison, 'Personal Views' in *BMJ* 319 (18 September 1999) p. 793 –

bmj.bmjjournals.com/cgi/content/full/319/7212/793

25 'End of Life', programme three of *Inside the Ethics Committee*, BBC Radio 4, 28 May 2005 – www.bbc.co.uk/radio4/science/ethicscommittee_tr3.shtml

26 'End of Life'

27 Pablo Rodríguez del Pozo and Joseph J. Fins, 'Death, dying and informatics: misrepresenting religion on Medline' in *BMC Medical Ethics* 6:6 (1 July 2005) – www.biomedcentral.com/1472-6939/6/6

28 www.ethicsforschools.org

29 Del Pozo and Fins, 'Death, dying and informatics: misrepresenting religion on Medline'

30 Jacobs, *Body Trauma TV*, p. 126

31 Jacobs, *Body Trauma TV*, p. 113

You can't make choices on what you think other people's expectations will be.

Steve Carell

7. *My Sister's Keeper* – Study Guide

Louise Crook

Book Title: My Sister's Keeper
Author: Jodi Picoult
UK Publisher: Atria Books (hardback); Hodder & Stoughton (paperback)
UK Publication Dates: 1 April 2004 (hardback); 10 January 2005 (paperback)

Quotations taken from UK paperback (Hodder & Stoughton, 2005) edition

Key Themes

Life, death, freedom, autonomy, suffering, fear, illness, parenting

Summary

Thirteen-year-old Anna Fitzgerald has been in and out of hospital since she was born. She has undergone many procedures and operations. But she isn't sick; her older sister Kate is. Kate has been battling with leukaemia since the age of two, and Anna was conceived through IVF in order to be a perfect donor for Kate. She is a genetically chosen child. Kate is now sixteen, and all the treatment she has received has led to kidney failure. After receiving her sister's platelets, blood and bone marrow, now there are even plans for her to have one of Anna's kidneys.

Having a sister who is always in and out of hospital has made it difficult for Anna to make friends, so she sticks closely to her family and considers Kate to be her best friend. Kate is always the centre of attention, however, and Anna is fed up with not being noticed. She and her older brother Jesse feel marginalised, leading to Jesse developing serious behavioural problems. Anna desperately wants to be loved and noticed for her own sake, and she also wants to be able to make her own decisions. As the medical procedures become increasingly invasive, Anna decides that she does not want to be a medical donor any longer. She no longer wants to be someone whose worth seems to be found only in making her sister better. She takes the dramatic step of applying for medical emancipation from her parents, so that only she has the right to decide what happens to her body.

Anna instructs the lawyer Campbell Alexander to fight her cause. Campbell has his own struggles, insecurities and secrets; the mystery of his inability to be separated from his faithful dog Judge is one example of his attempt to shut out the world. As Anna is a minor, Julia Romano is appointed as her *guardian ad litem* to help her through the court process. Campbell and Julia have a history of their own which unfolds as the story progresses, revealing the deep hurt and anxiety that they have both experienced.

This legal battle threatens to pull the Fitzgerald family apart. Sara and Brian Fitzgerald are dedicated parents who want what is best for their family. Anna is living under their roof and is their daughter, yet her proposed action will effectively end their other daughter's life. Brian is a fire fighter whose job is to save people, which compounds his frustration at being unable to save his daughter. Sara is a former lawyer who has given up her career to look after her family, but now finds herself unexpectedly caught up in a legal battle. Both of them feel helpless – as does Jesse, their neglected older child who is turning to arson. It is almost impossible for Brian and Sara to decide on the best course of action for their family. The revelation at the end of the novel about Anna's true motive for desiring medical emancipation adds further confusion to the family relationships.

My Sister's Keeper is narrated by five characters with their different perspectives. It is a thought-provoking novel filled with profound moral choices and heartache.

Background

Jodi Picoult grew up in Nesconset, New York, and was educated at both Princeton and Harvard Universities. At 38 years old, she has already written eleven novels, many of which deal with controversial topics. *Mercy* (1996) is about euthanasia; *The Pact* (1998) deals with teenage suicide; and *Keeping Faith* (1999) is about child abuse in the Catholic church. Her other novels are *Harvesting the Heart* (1993), *Picture Perfect* (1995), *Plain Truth* (2000), *Salem Falls* (2001), *Perfect Match* (2002), *Second Glance* (2003) and *Vanishing Acts* (2005). Her latest novel, *The Tenth Circle*, was published in April 2006. Picoult has been extremely popular in the USA since *Songs of the Humpback Whale* hit the shelves in 1992. Her success in the UK has been much slower, and it was not until 2005 when *My Sister's Keeper* was selected as one of Richard and Judy's Best Reads on Channel 4's *Richard and Judy Show* that she became a well-known author on this side of the Atlantic.

Jodi Picoult is married with three children, and says that her experience as a mother, wife and family member significantly shapes her writing. In an interview with *BookEnds*, she explains what inspired her to tackle such a difficult subject in *My Sister's Keeper*:

> I had been working on an earlier book, *Second Glance*, which was in part about the Vermont Eugenics project and, basically, a period of time in America when we were dabbling in racial hygiene, like the Nazis. As I studied eugenics, I kept turning up the story of an American couple that had conceived a child as a bone marrow match for a sibling with a rare cancer. The ill child had been in remission for four years – four years longer than she was expected to live; the brother's stem cells had been procured from his umbilical cord blood (something we routinely throw away in the US). I started to wonder what would happen if that sister went out of remission – if the brother would feel responsible. I wondered what would happen if it weren't a one time donation, but several painful ones. And I wondered what it would be like to grow up wondering if you'd been born only because your sister was ill. That became the beginning of *My Sister's Keeper*.[1]

Questions for Discussion

1. What did you think of *My Sister's Keeper*? How did you feel as the story unfolded?

2. Which character do you sympathise with most and why? What does having the story told by five different narrators add to the book? Do you think Jodi Picoult is more sympathetic to some characters than to others? If so, which ones? Why?

3. How do you react to Anna as a character? How would you describe her? Why is she so confused about issuing the lawsuit? How does your understanding of her change as the story progresses?

4. Why do you think Jesse has such behavioural problems? What do you think of the methods his family use to deal with these?

5. What is your opinion of Sara? Why is she so desperate to keep Kate alive? Do you think she treats her other children as second best, and if so why?

6. Why are Sara and Brian always questioning whether they have done a good job as parents? What makes them feel so inadequate? What is it that makes many parents in our society feel like this?

7. Why are the members of the Fitzgerald family so isolated from each other? What stops them relating openly and honestly to each other? How do they deal with their responsibility for, and dependence on, each other?

8. What does *My Sister's Keeper* have to say about family discord? What does the Bible have to teach about family relationships (see, for example, Ex. 20:12; Pr. 23:22–25; Eph. 5:21–6:4)? How might this teaching be relevant here?

9. Campbell Alexander admits that, 'Out of necessity – medical and emotional – I have gotten rather skilled at being an escape artist.' (p. 279)

   Why do you think Campbell hides his illness? What else is he hiding from? Why? To what extent is Julia also hiding, and how does this impact their relationship?

10. Do you think that it is morally right to do whatever it takes to save a child's life – even if that means infringing on the life of another? How does *My Sister's Keeper* deal with this central moral question? What does the Bible have to say about this to guide our thinking (see, for example, Gen. 4:8–12; Job 34:14–15; Lk. 12:4–7)?

11. What does this novel show about our culture's promotion of individual rights? What does God teach us about our human rights (see, for example, Lev. 19:32–36; Ps. 72:1–4; Is. 10:1–4; Gal. 3:26–29)? How does this differ from the prevalent view in our culture?

12. How did you feel about the final outcome of the case? Do you think justice was done according to our society's standards, and as God would define justice? How does the end of the novel change your perspective on the trial outcome?

13. How does Jodi Picoult deal with the ethical and moral issues related to Anna being a 'designer

baby'? What are the ethical and moral implications of this genetic selection? What conclusions have you reached about such medical technology? How does your belief in God, and the knowledge that we are all created in his image (Gen. 1:26–27; Ps. 8:3–8) affect your views on this?

14. What similar real-life moral and ethical dilemmas about the end and preservation of life can you think of? How can we apply the Bible to these situations? How can Christians respond to these cases to show the importance of knowing God and his purposes for our world (see, for example, Col. 1:15–23; Rev. 21:1–5)?

15. At the beginning of the novel, Campbell and Anna briefly discuss the idea of suing God. What role does God play in *My Sister's Keeper*? How might Christian faith have made a difference to each of the characters (see, for example, Rom. 5:1–5; 8:28–39; 1 Pet. 1:3–7)? How might knowledge of God make a difference in the lives of your non-Christian friends and family?

16. *My Sister's Keeper* is a novel overshadowed by death and the threat of death. How do the members of the Fitzgerald family cope with this? Do you think they have considered what will happen to Kate after she dies, or whether there is life after death? How do you think this novel reflects the fear of death that exists in our society? What does the Bible teach us about death (see Ecc. 3:1–8,18–21; Jn. 5:24–30; 1 Cor. 15:21–28,42–58; Heb. 9:27)? How could you relate to this fear of death in sharing the good news of Jesus Christ with your friends?

Notes

1 Harry Doherty, 'The BookEnds Interview: Jodi Picoult', *BookEnds* –
www.thebookplace.com/bookends/be_interviews_picoult.asp?TAG=&CID=

We are the products of evolution, not of some grand design which says this is what we are and that's it ... People say we are playing God. My answer is: 'If we don't play God, who will?'

James Watson

8. *The Island* – Study Guide

Tony Watkins

Film Title: The Island
Tagline: They don't want you to know what you are.
Director: Michael Bay
Screenplay: Caspian Tredwell-Owen, Alex Kurtzman, Roberto Orci
Starring: Ewan McGregor, Scarlett Johansson, Sean Bean, Steve Buscemi, Djimon Hounsou
Distributor: Warner Brothers
Cinema Release Date: 12 August 2005
DVD Release Date: 9 January 2006
DVD Certificate: 15

Key Themes

Human nature, life, death, ethics, cloning, medical technology, health, freedom, science, God

Summary

Lincoln Six Echo (Ewan McGregor) wakes from another nightmare. His room is cold and clinical, and displays on the wall of his room report his 'erratic REM sleep cycle' as well as increased sodium levels in his urine. He is to report to the Tranquillity Centre for a 'wellness examination'. He dresses in a white jump-suit and leaves his room, joining other identically-dressed inhabitants of the Merrick Institute under the watchful eyes of security guards dressed in black. Announcements instruct the inhabitants to, 'Remember: be polite, pleasant and peaceful. A healthy person is a happy person.' They all appear fit and healthy thanks to the gym and a swimming pool. Many, particularly women, are young and attractive, and a significant proportion of these women are pregnant. But there are disturbing elements, too: children's cartoons play on the screens around the walls, and a group of men are reading a very simple children's book aloud and in unison. There are, however, no children anywhere in sight. Diet is monitored and strictly controlled, but Lincoln Six Echo's best friend Jordan Two Delta (Scarlett Johansson) manages to sweet-talk the woman serving breakfast into giving her some bacon, which she then gives to Lincoln. Their jobs appear to be connected with sophisticated biotechnology, but their roles are extremely monotonous.

Everyone believes that they are survivors of a major global catastrophe which has left the outside world contaminated. They can never go outside and never see daylight, except through vast windows all around their tower, which enable them to view a beautiful far-off island – 'nature's last remaining pathogen-free zone'. Each day there is a lottery to see which, if any, lucky winner will be fortunate enough to go to the Island and be allowed to live in the open again. When the expectant mothers go into labour, they leave for the Island immediately.

However, Lincoln Six Echo is not happy with this simple, protected life. When he reports to Doctor Merrick (Sean Bean) for his check up, he asks a torrent of questions about why their existence is as it is: Why does everyone have to wear white? Who folds his clothes? Who decided that everybody here likes tofu? What is tofu, anyway? Why can't he eat bacon for breakfast? 'I want to know answers,' he says, 'and I wish, I wish that there was more.' 'More?' asks Doctor Merrick. 'More than just waiting to go to the Island,' is Lincoln Six Echo's response. Merrick seems disturbed by this curiosity and tells him that he needs to run some tests – in particular a synaptic brain scan.

Later, Lincoln Six Echo pretends his computer has broken so he can go to see a friend, 'Mac' McCord (Steve Buscemi), who works in the service area, off limits to the white-suited inhabitants unless they wear protective suits. Mac is very different from Lincoln Six Echo's other friends: hard-bitten, cynical, and very worried about the consequences of his conversations with Lincoln being discovered. While visiting Mac, Lincoln sees a butterfly – the first non-human living creature he has ever seen. He catches it in a matchbox belonging to Mac. Later, he tells Jordan Two Delta that he has a feeling something is wrong. The 'bug' should not even survive outside, never mind be able to get into the service area of the supposedly contamination-proof institute. And why was Jordan's file open on Merrick's computer when Lincoln went in to see him earlier that morning?

During the night, Lincoln returns the butterfly to where he found it in the service area. He decides to follow it and ends up witnessing two very disturbing incidents. First, he sees a mother who had gone into labour earlier in the day being given a lethal injection as soon as she has given birth. Then, he is startled to see the winner of the most recent lottery running down the corridor, dripping blood, trailing wires and tubes, and screaming, 'I don't want to die.' We see what Lincoln doesn't: that the baby has been given to an identical mother and her husband, and that the lottery winner's organs were being removed to be transplanted into his double, a famous American football player. The white-suited inhabitants of the Merrick Institute are all clones.

When Jordan wins the lottery, Lincoln finds her and persuades her to escape with him. They head out through the service area, with security in hot pursuit. Before they finally reach the outside world, they discover that the ocean – and the Island – which they had always seen through the Institute windows, are nothing but a holographic projection. It looks as though some catastrophe may have happened – they are in an arid, scrubby desert with no signs of life anywhere. After running for some time, they come to a road and follow it until they reach the bar advertised on Mac's matchbox. They find Mac inside and he takes them to his home, where he can explain things to them privately:

> **Lincoln:** Why do they lie to us?
> **Mac:** To stop you knowing what you are.
> **Lincoln and Jordan:** What are we?
> **Mac:** Why do I have to be the guy who tells the kids there's no Santa Claus. . . . You're not like me. You're not human. You're not *real* like me. You're clones. . . . Everyone wants to live forever – it's the new American Dream.

They persuade Mac to help them, and he takes them to catch a train to Los Angeles where Lincoln can find his 'sponsor' – the person who had him cloned as a source of spare parts. Meanwhile, Albert Laurent and his team of mercenaries, having been hired by Merrick to find the two clones, are on their trail. Mac is killed at the station, but Lincoln and Jordan manage to escape onto the train. They are picked up by the police in LA when they use Mac's credit card. The police call up Lincoln's file on their in-car computer. It is, of course, the record of his sponsor, Tom Lincoln. Lincoln Six Echo sees the address and, when he and Jordan escape in the confusion caused by Laurent's team attacking the police, they go to find him.

Tom Lincoln is a wealthy designer and a playboy suffering from cirrhotic hepatitis – 'a parting gift from God for all my philandering'. Lincoln Six Echo apparently persuades Tom to help, but the sponsor really intends to return his 'insurance policy' to the Institute. They set off in Tom's car but are chased and eventually trapped by Laurent. As Laurent holds them both at gunpoint, he cannot tell which is the clone. Lincoln Six Echo snaps his Merrick Institute bracelet onto Tom's wrist and Laurent shoots him. Lincoln Six Echo returns to the Institute as Tom, ostensibly to have samples taken for a new clone. Jordan Two Delta gets herself picked up by Laurent so that she, too, can get back to the Institute. They plan to disable the holographic system and reveal the truth. Lincoln eventually succeeds, though not before Merrick catches him, while Jordan sets free a group of clones. She is surprised to find Laurent helping her, the bounty-hunter having concluded that what Merrick was doing was wrong. Ultimately, Merrick is killed, the Institute destroyed, and all the clones go free.

Background

The Island is directed by Michael Bay – no stranger to explosive stunts and special effects, having previously made *Bad Boys* (1995), *The Rock* (1996), *Armageddon* (1998), *Pearl Harbour* (2001) and *Bad Boys II* (2003). The story was written by Caspian Tredwell-Owen whose only significant writing previously had been for *Beyond Borders* (2003). His screenplay was further developed by Alex Kurtzman and Roberto Orci who also worked together on *The Legend of Zorro* (2005) and *Mission Impossible III* (2006). One of the crucial changes they made was making Jordan Two Delta a much more robust and capable character rather than the vulnerable 'damsel in distress' of the original screenplay.

The Island features a very high level of product placement – Puma shoes for the inhabitants of the Merrick Institute, X-Box entertainment for the Institute inhabitants, prominent branding of MSN on an 'information point' in LA, and much more besides. The most interesting of these blurs the boundary between fact and fiction: a real-life Calvin Klein poster and TV/film advert featuring Scarlett Johansson are used in the film. When Jordan Two Delta sees them, she realises that the model is her sponsor, Sarah Jordan. At least in some cinemas, the Calvin Klein advert was included among the other adverts before the film started.

The film was criticised for being too much of an action movie while toying with big ethical and philosophical questions. Olly Richards, for example, writes:

> Bay being Bay, he doesn't really delve much into the psychology of discovering that you're a human facsimile or that nothing you remember is real. There are hints of it: born into physical adulthood, the clones learn at the rate of newborns, questioning their surroundings as they get older. But such internal troubles lose out to the external and are too often brushed away.[1]

Bay wanted people to begin to think about the issues raised in an enjoyable action film, rather than have the film completely issue-led. He says, 'It's a universal theme of this movie that we all want to live longer. It's just how far you would go.'[2]

Questions for Discussion

1. How well do you feel Michael Bay balanced the exploration of big themes with the action and effects? What, for you, are the strongest and weakest points?

2. What did you think of the extensive product placement? Did this affect your viewing of the film? How?

3. What would you identify as the key themes which are touched on? To what extent do you feel the film really deals with the questions it raises?

4. Lincoln's synaptic scan shows significant and surprising development of his brain – with the memories of Tom Lincoln. What is suggested through this, and other parts of the film, about where we get our knowledge from?

5. 'The human organism. Unique in all the universe in its complexity. The product of three billion years of evolution. Perfect in every way except one. Like all machines it wears out. . . . in compliance with the eugenics laws of 2015, all our agnates are maintained in a persistent vegetative state. They never achieve consciousness. They never think or suffer or feel pain, joy, love, hate. It's a product,

ladies and gentlemen, in every way that matters. Not human.' (Dr Merrick to potential customers)

What does *The Island* say about the value of human life? To what extent is the film consistent with this position in its use of violence? How does the film's view of human value compare with the Bible's (see, for example, Ps. 8; Mk. 12:29–31)?

6. What was the ethical basis for Dr Merrick's actions? What do you think *The Island* is ultimately saying about human cloning? How do you respond to this as a Christian (see, for example, 1 Cor. 6:19–20; 2 Cor. 4:7–18; 12:9)?

7. Is Jordan right or wrong to preserve her own existence at the expense of Sarah Jordan's life? Why/why not?

8. What do you think Tom Lincoln should have done when his 'insurance policy' turned up at his house? Is Lincoln Six Echo right or wrong to clip his Merrick Institute bracelet onto Tom's wrist as they face the gun barrel of Albert Laurent? Why/why not?

9. At what point does Albert Laurent (Djimon Hounsou) change his mind? Why does he do so? In what ways does this echo the concern for the well-being of slaves seen in Ex. 21:20–21,26–27 and Lev. 25:39–43,54–55?

10. Did the clones have a right to know the truth about their situation? Why/why not?

11. **Lincoln Six Echo:** What's with Merrick?
Mac: . . . It's called a God-complex. All doctors are like that. They think they know everything.

Lincoln: What's God?

Mac: You know when you want something really bad, and you close your eyes and wish for it? God's the guy who ignores you.

What is the film's view of God and of spiritual aspects of life? What is the significance of the statue of the broken angel being featured so prominently in the scene when Laurent comes upon Tom Lincoln and his clone fighting each other?

12. 'You're special. You have a very special purpose in life. You've been chosen. The Island awaits you.' [voice during the agnate conditioning process]

Lincoln: I want to know answers. And I wish that there was more.

Merrick: More?

Lincoln: Yeah. More than just waiting to go to the Island.

In what ways does the Island work as a metaphor for heaven? What does Jordan mean when she says, 'The Island is real. It's us.' What, if anything, is this suggesting about the human hope for heaven? How does this compare with what the Bible says (see, for example, Is. 65:17–25; Rev. 21:22–22:5)?

13. How did you feel about the scenes in which Merrick is killed and the clones finally see the real world? In what ways do the destruction of the Merrick Institute and the release of the clones parallel the biblical picture of the final triumph of Christ and the day of resurrection (see Rev. 20:11–15)?

Notes

[1] Olly Richards, 'The Island', *Empire Online* – www.empireonline.com/athome/movies/review.asp?ID=116930

[2] Jeff Otto, 'Interview: Michael Bay and Scarlett Johansson', *IGN FilmForce* – filmforce.ign.com/articles/635/635158p3.html

It's not who you are underneath. It's what you do that defines you.

Rachel Dawes in the film *Batman Begins*

9. Life After God? The Ethical Teaching of Peter Singer

Dr Peter May

Peter Singer is arguably the most famous and influential modern philosopher, offering the most radical challenge to traditional Judeo-Christian values. It has been said of him, that as an original and influential moral pioneer, he surpasses any philosopher since Bertrand Russell. On his website he says, 'My work is based on the assumption that clarity and consistency in our moral thinking is likely, in the long run, to lead us to hold better views on ethical issues.'

Born in Australia in 1946, Peter Singer is the son of Jews who fled from Vienna to avoid persecution from the Nazis. His grandparents and other relatives, who stayed behind, were killed. His mother was a doctor. His father, a keen animal lover, was a businessman. Studying initially in Melbourne, Singer went on to obtain a PhD in Philosophy at Oxford, where he also developed his concerns for the well-being of animals. Subsequently, he taught in Oxford, New York, Colorado and California. He then returned to Melbourne to become Professor in Human Bioethics. In 1999 he became Professor of Bioethics at the Center for Human Values at Princeton University.

Peter Singer is a prolific writer on ethics and related areas of philosophy. His best known book, *Animal Liberation: A New Ethic for Our Treatment of Animals* (1976),[1] gave birth to the worldwide animal rights movement, promoting enormous interest in vegetarianism. He has written many other books, a major entry on ethics in *Encyclopaedia Britannica* and countless journal and review articles, as well as editing influential journals. Much of what follows is focused on his book *How Are We To Live?*[2] with various references to other writings.

His Broad Perspective

Singer is an atheist who very easily dismisses Judeo-Christian ethics as being out of date and irrelevant: 'We have no need to postulate gods who hand down commandments to us because we understand ethics as a natural phenomenon.'[3] He asks, 'What do I think of as a good life in the fullest sense of that term? This is an ultimate question.'[4] The choice is ours because, in Singer's view, ethical principles are not laws written up in heaven. Nor are they absolute truths about the universe, known by intuition. The principles of ethics come from our own nature as social, reasoning beings. So, 'We are free to choose what we are to be, because we have no essential nature, that is, no given purpose outside ourselves. Unlike say, an apple tree that has come into existence as a result of someone else's plan, we simply exist, and the rest is up to us.'[5]

His principle reason for rejecting the Christian God is the existence of suffering in the world. In particular, he dismisses the idea that mankind is distinct from other animals by being made in the image of God. Hence the 'Sanctity of Human Life' argument, which hangs on that distinctive, goes out of the window. All that remains are 'Quality of Life' issues. This leads him to the utilitarian principle of 'The greatest happiness for the greatest number', which undergirds so much modern political thought.[6] Pleasure (or, rather, 'preference satisfaction') becomes the greatest good; suffering and pain the only evils. Utilitarianism, therefore, invites an examination of the consequences of our actions, studying the effects of our choices on others. Our actions themselves have no intrinsic moral value – what matters is what happens. Our intentions count for nothing; the starting point is preference not motivation. Reducing ethical choices to a concern for personal preferences and useful consequences sounds like a simplification of life's moral dilemmas. However, the ethical process involved in arriving at such a decision can be extremely complicated:

> I must, if I am thinking ethically, imagine myself in the situation of all those affected by my action (with the preferences that they have). I must consider the interests of my enemies as well as my friends, and of strangers as well as family. Only if, after taking fully into account the interests and preferences of all these people, I still think the action is better than any alternative open to me, can I genuinely say that I ought to do it. At the same time I must not ignore the long-term effects of fostering family ties, of establishing and promoting reciprocal relationships, and of allowing wrongdoers to benefit from their wrong doing.[7]

Abortion and Infanticide

Suffering is, of course, more than just the experience of pain. It has to do with self-conscious awareness of suffering, involving the memory of past freedom from suffering, understanding the causes of suffering, and anticipating the future implications and possible options. An unborn child cannot suffer in this way – and, of course, cannot be said to have personal preferences, whether or not they could ever be expressed. If other people have preferences that the unborn child should not survive, and assuming the procedure can be done painlessly, there remains no moral barrier to terminating the pregnancy:

> Those who regard the interests of women as overriding the merely potential interests of the foetus are taking their stand on a morally impregnable position.[8]

Furthermore, the situation is essentially unchanged for the newborn child who does not understand what life is about and therefore can have no preference in the matter. If no one else has a preference that the child should live, infanticide within the first month of life can be morally justified. Here Singer introduces his ethic of *replaceability*. A child may not be wanted for various reasons, such as timing, gender or congenital disease. The decision-making process can be profoundly influenced if the death of an unwanted child subsequently allows the parents the freedom to have a wanted child who would replace it. Such ethics have not endeared him to the disabled community in general. They fear that his views support discrimination against them. Neither have they gone down well in Germany with its painful memories of the eugenics movement for genetic purity.

Euthanasia – Voluntary and Non-Voluntary

Singer's overthrow of the 'Sanctity of Human Life Ethic', replacing it with a 'Quality of Life Ethic', comes most sharply into focus when considering voluntary euthanasia. This is most fully discussed in his book, *Rethinking Life and Death*, where he offers some new rules:[9]

Firstly, we should not see all human lives as of equal worth but recognise that some are more valuable than others. Such judgements should be made on the basis of the individual's capacity to think, relate and experience. Patients in a persistent vegetative state have none of these faculties. Without consciousness, life has no value. In cases of brain damage making it impossible for the patient to express a preference, this principle obviously opens the door to non-voluntary euthanasia.

Secondly, the taking of human life is not a moral issue in itself; the consequences of the action determine the ethical rightness of it. The preferences of the individual – if they can be expressed – are of central importance.

Thirdly, suicide is not intrinsically wrong. An individual's desire to die should be respected. Hence, it is ethical for a doctor to assist a suicide in fulfilling the patient's considered preference.

Animal Liberation and Vegetarianism

Singer distinguishes *human beings* in the biological sense from *persons*, who are rational and self-conscious beings. He has no basis for seeing human beings in a different category from other animals. In general, humans have more intelligence and greater self-awareness, but some humans lack these faculties. In the newborn they are undeveloped; in the severely brain damaged they are lost; and in the dementing they are fading day by day. They are humans, but not persons. Some adult animals, however, are remarkably intelligent. They are persons, though not human.

More important for Singer is the division between sentient creatures, which can experience pleasure and suffering, and non-sentient creatures which cannot. Most – but not all – humans come in the first category, as do many animals. Hence the protection afforded to persons should be extended to such non-humans. The division between these categories is not always obvious.[10] Some animals even seem to demonstrate a moral awareness by altruistic behaviour. He cites dolphins helping injured dolphins to breathe, wolves taking food back to the pack, chimpanzees calling others when they find ripe fruit, and gazelles putting their own lives at risk by warning of predators.[11]

The focus of Singer's concern about animals is the human tendency to think in terms of species. While sexism and racism assert the superiority of one sex or race over another, *speciesism* asserts that humans are superior to other animals. Such discrimination, in Singer's view, is indefensible.[12] His philosophy not only rules out all cruelty to self-conscious, sentient beings, which includes adult mammals, but also rules out their killing. Fur coats and leather shoes cannot then be justified, and neither, in general, can eating meat.[13] If animal experimentation can ever be justified, then it must be equally justifiable to perform such experiments on severely mentally-retarded human adults, or normal infants who are not aware of what is being done to them.[14]

Sexuality

'The moral case for acceptance of sexual relationships between consenting adults that do not harm others is

. . . clear-cut.'[15] As long as the consequences of sexual acts fulfil the preferences of those involved and do not harm others, sexual ethics are of little or no importance. The important ethical issues in the world today, he continues, are the fact that racial hatred stops people living together, that people are starving in an affluent world, that animals are bred in factory farms, and that we are damaging the ecological system of our planet:

> Once it is generally understood that ethics has no necessary connection with the sexually-obsessed morality of conservative Christianity, a humane and positive ethic could be the basis for a renewal of our social, political and ecological life.[16]

In a review article entitled *Heavy Petting*,[17] Singer asks what is wrong with human sexual activity with animals. The argument that bestiality is unnatural because it cannot lead to procreation is not good enough, he says, because many widely practised sexual activities, which are seen to be natural, cannot lead to procreation either. Isn't bestiality cruel and harmful? Not necessarily. Can animals meaningfully give consent to sex? Well, sometimes they initiate it, as for instance a dog rubbing its genitals against a human leg. If the animal shows a preference and there are no harmful consequences, there appear to be no grounds in Singer's ethical framework to object.

World Poverty

Singer castigates Christians for their attitude to world poverty.[18] He sees a major discrepancy between their passion for the sanctity of life argument as it relates to the embryo, the unwanted infant and the terminally ill, and their failure to take seriously – in his view – Christ's teaching about possessions and the needs of the poor. He sees Christians being concerned for those who express no desire to live while ignoring the lives of countless people who long to hang on to life. Christ's teaching to the rich young ruler is certainly stark, and the wealth of western Christians is disturbingly great.

Critique of Singer on Christianity

Singer finds it easy not to take Christianity seriously:

> Once we admit that Darwin was right when he argued that human ethics evolved from the social instincts that we inherited from our non-human ancestors, we can put aside the hypothesis of a divine origin for ethics.[19]

He has not written a substantial critique of Christianity, but his general antipathy is clear. He does not understand the dynamics of the gospel of grace, and so has a 'salvation by works' understanding of Christian theology, where ethical behaviour is driven by self-interest in rewards[20] and fear of punishments.[21] He is left with 'a man of straw' to knock down – or rather, marginalise.

Central to his concerns is speciesism and the Judeo-Christian view that mankind is made uniquely in the image of God. He emphasises the Bible's view that humanity has been given dominion over the animals. This he always describes in terms of dominating rule, never as responsible, caring stewardship. Christians, however, do not believe that animals are their possession, to do with as they think fit. Singer emphasises Genesis

1:28 which speaks of 'rule', but ignores Genesis 2 which introduces the ideas of a 'duty of care' and also companionship. In fact, there are many references in the Bible to the well-being of animals, which Singer chooses to ignore. They qualify and describe how 'dominion' over the animals is to be expressed.[22]

In the New Testament, Jesus pointed to God's provision for the birds, but in saying that people are more valuable than they are, he is clearly not saying that they are without value before God.[23] Singer clearly does not like the way that Jesus cast out demons and sent them into a herd of pigs,[24] but he ignores the significance of Christ challenging the legalism of the Pharisees by asking, 'If one of you has a son or an ox that falls into a well on the Sabbath day, will you not immediately pull him out?'[25] Graham Cole comments that juxtaposing a child at risk and an ox at risk indicates the expanse of Christ's circle of compassion.[26] Cole also notes that in his letters, Paul describes God's ultimate purposes for the whole of creation[27] which Singer fails to consider. In other words, Singer's treatment of Scripture is misleading – perhaps unethical. He selects proof texts to support his argument, without trying to see them in their wider context.

Critique of Singer's Utilitarianism

There are several well-documented difficulties with utilitarian philosophy.[28]

1. Consequences

The intellectual challenge of chess is to think through the implications of a move and predict the knock-on effects. A move you think is brilliant may prove a short cut to being in checkmate. The game must be played slowly. The difficulty is that we cannot cope with too many possible alternatives, which is why most of us play chess badly! Only God can see the future; the rest of us have to settle for shrewd guesses. One amusing story about Singer is that he fed a vegetarian diet to his cat – with the result that the cat became very skilled at catching mice! According to Craig and Moreland, the consequences by which the action is to be judged have, 'an uncertainty that paralyses moral decision-making.' Furthermore, it 'brings to centre stage a tentativeness about duty that is not conducive to the development of conviction and character'.[29]

Consider the consequences of sexual activity. Commonly regarded as harmless pleasure, it is far from easy to predict the implications of a given sexual encounter, either emotionally or physically. The consequences of an unwanted pregnancy should be obvious enough, but are frequently overlooked. Many, presumably to their great surprise, have found themselves quickly addicted to a new sexual partner or a behaviour pattern that becomes very destructive to them and their families. Infection – often leading to infertility or cervical cancer – commonly occurs, but rarely seems to be anticipated. The single greatest cause of pain and suffering in the world today is due to the devastation brought by the sexual transmission of HIV, which does not even feature in Singer's list of 'the crucial moral questions of our day'.[30] How could he overlook it? We do not know how the virus crossed from monkeys to humans; whatever happened, the consequences could not have been imagined. Less surprising is his failure to even begrudgingly acknowledge that the only practice that could resolve the epidemic (and do so within a generation) is the biblical ideal of one sexual partner for life.

2. Happiness

Each attempt to explain the principle of utilitarianism presents its own difficulties. The best known description is that it seeks 'the greatest happiness for the greatest number'. Two issues immediately arise that may well be in conflict.

Imagine that I have £1,000,000 to give away. If I was concerned for the greatest happiness, I might decide to give it all to one person. However, if I was concerned for the greatest number, I might give £1 to each of a million people. Many would not even consider thanking me! Yet one might think that giving away money would be among the simpler moral decisions.

But there is a second, more fundamental problem. What exactly is happiness? And if I knew, how might I obtain it and hold on to it? Those who experience the most intense happiness find they cannot maintain it. It inevitably fades. Similarly, those who experience the deepest tragedies seem, in the passage of time, to recover and once more find things to smile about. It is an extraordinary feature of life that some of the poorest people are among the most contented, while some of the wealthiest are among the most wretched. This is true of individuals, but it is also true of societies: 'Ghana, Mexico, Sweden, the United Kingdom and the United States all share similar life satisfaction scores despite per capita income varying ten-fold between the richest and the poorest country.'[31] If happiness is so poorly correlated to wealth, the same study, among others, shows that it *is* strongly correlated to the traditional family unit. The divorce rate in Britain has quadrupled since 1970, and currently 40,000 children a year are prescribed anti-depressants. Therefore, one might suppose that the morality of actions that undermine the family unit, cannot be advocated on utilitarian grounds – again underlining the central importance of sexual ethics.

3. Reductionism

Preference consequentialism seems a flat earth way of doing ethics. The whole process is reduced to a two-dimensional view of life: our actions are evaluated only in terms of their consequences (whether or not they are actually predictable or measurable). There is no recognition of ultimate goodness, no acknowledgement of the importance of motive, no significance attached to the agonies of conscience or the depths of moral revulsion, no sense of overall meaning and purpose, no exploration of the nature of self-denying love rather than 'preference satisfaction', no realisation of the need for forgiveness, no understanding of the fallibility of human moral character and no basis for considering justice. Nor does Singer allow the subtle influences of our relationships in moral decision making, even though his own rationality proved an insufficient guide in dealing with his mother's death from Alzheimer's disease.[32] Morality is evaluated only on the consequences of our actions, but most of us realise that there is rather more going on as we make our choices.

4. The Yuk Factor[33]

In his letter to the Romans, Paul teaches that certain truths about right behaviour are instinctive. We don't need to be taught them, but if we suppress such intuitive awareness, it will affect our rational grasp of ethical judgements.[34] We will become 'futile in our thinking.'

Several aspects of Singer's teaching cause deep intuitive revulsion – not just in Christians, but in people who make many different assumptions about the nature of truth and ethics. Singer claims the taboos are falling one by one[35] (late abortion, infanticide in the first month of life, non-voluntary euthanasia and bestiality are four such categories, which he clearly advocates). However, there are some taboos he seems reluctant to discuss. Given his grounds for justifying sexual activities between consenting adults, how can he raise adequate objections to promiscuity or, indeed, prostitution?[36] And what about incest, if there are no harmful consequences and both parties desire it? As there is no internationally-agreed age at which children become adults, he is also left without strong grounds for condemning paedophilia. Why is he so quiet about that explosive subject? Is it not another major, modern, ethical issue? What has he got to say about it?

5. Is it liveable?

Gordon Preece maintains that preference utilitarianism is actually unliveable: Singer's demanding universal utilitarianism is much more opposed to individual pleasure and almost infinitely guilt-inducing compared to Christianity.[37] The problems of the entire world are set before us. And it is not just the greatest happiness for the greatest number of humans which must direct our moral choices, but of all sentient mammals. The task is overwhelming.

Of course, the demands of world poverty distress us all. Historically, however, it has never been like this. In apostolic times, for instance, a church community might learn from a traveller about a distant fellowship experiencing hard times, and collect some money to help them. In general, they remained entirely ignorant of the human condition worldwide. For the most part, people lived in small, self-contained communities within which they learned to carry one another's burdens.[38] In such communities, the New Testament asserts our primary responsibility for our immediate family,[39] but then to care for widows and orphans,[40] to show hospitality to strangers[41] and, as opportunity arises, to do good to everyone.[42] In all this, the family is central. As the fundamental building block of society, it is without rival. Certainly states should provide welfare, but who would prefer institutionalised care? Any philosophy or political policy which damages or undermines the integrity of the family unit, as Singer does in dismissing the importance of sexual ethics, undermines the central structure of care in the community throughout the world. His quest for a renewal of our social and political life, disconnected from traditional sexual ethics, is a pipe-dream.[43]

Today, however, the tragedies of the world find their way onto the screens in our living rooms. We are not absolved responsibility for how we respond,[44] but the New Testament is realistic saying that we should 'not grow weary of doing good . . . as we have opportunity.'[45] We are not to lay up treasures on earth but in heaven,[46] and hard choices face each of us. For all that Christians say in criticizing our consumerist society, we still drive expensive cars, make our homes very comfortable and fly around the world for pleasure with seemingly little concern. So we should take note of Singer's serious challenge for Christians to behave Christianly.[47]

Yet utilitarianism gives us no respite. If we were to take Singer at face value, our lives would be minimalist. We could hardly waste money buying books of any sort; education would be basic and presumably prevent the sort of expensive researches which might lead to significant benefits for the world's poor. We could forget about the arts and entertainment – luxuries no one should afford. In order to remain sane with such pressing demands, Singer apparently gives away 20 per cent of his income. This is impressive, and certainly puts many Christians to shame.[48] But given the needs of the world, the figure is quite arbitrary. If you have a large income, far more than enough to supply your basic needs, why not make it 50 per cent? However, on consequentialist thinking, any such self-inflicted poverty/misery is endured to bring the greatest amount of happiness to the greatest number. Is it defeating your primary objectives to advocate miserly restraint? So we return to some very basic questions. Perhaps we should not give away more than we are happy to give, so that we don't add to the pot of suffering.

At the end of the day, we can understand the idea of acting morally towards the people we meet. It is more difficult to act morally to those we do not know. Acting morally to everyone in the world is quite beyond us, but acting morally and equally to every sentient mammal robs morality of any real meaning. The best we can do is respond as and when we have the opportunity. Christians have grounds for believing that God is ultimately responsible for his world, but has put us in caring and supportive family units so that we might be agents of his mercy and compassion.

The Point of View of the Universe

Jesus took as the central plank of his ethical teaching, the Old Testament commandment, 'You should love your neighbour as yourself.'[49] Not surprisingly, he was then asked the crucial question, 'Who is my neighbour?' In answering it, Jesus told one of the world's greatest stories: 'A certain man went down from Jerusalem to Jericho . . .'[50] The despised foreigner from Samaria is cast as the rescuer, going out of his way to help the injured man at significant personal inconvenience and cost – he is the true neighbour. Singer sees the commandment, with Christ's explanation as to who our neighbour is, as a universal ethic. It is also expressed as Christ's 'golden rule' that you should, 'Do for others what you would like them do for you.'[51] Singer claims it lifts us from our subjective, personal point of view to a wider, objective perspective, encouraging equal consideration of interests, ultimately even 'the point of view of the universe'.[52] In supporting this idea, he appeals to 'all the major ethical traditions', naming Rabbinic Judaism, Hinduism and the teaching of Confucius, who 'appear to have reached the same position independently of each other.'[53] What he fails to notice is that Christ alone puts the golden rule in the positive form. All the others say, in effect, that you should *not* do to others what you would *not* want them to do to you. That, it seems, is the wisdom of the world: it concerns what you shouldn't do, not what you should do. What Christ taught was unique.

In the modern world of instant communications about the most awful disasters, Christ's golden rule may seem overwhelming. However, acknowledging our failings to a gracious God, finding his forgiveness, realising that he understands our limitations, opening ourselves up to his good purposes, realising that 'each day has enough trouble of its own',[54] and also that this is God's world and not ours, the Christian is not overwhelmed – either by guilt or the size of the task. Christ's way is possible; Singer's is crushing.

Conclusion

In dismissing Christianity, Singer recognises that he has been unable to find a higher ethic than Christ's, but is less than persuaded that he has found a compelling alternative as a basis for such ethical thinking. He writes:

> Ethical truths are not written into the fabric of the universe ... If there were no beings with desires or preferences of any kind, nothing would be of value and ethics would lack all content.[55]

However, there are not only the subjective values of each individual:

> The possibility of being led, by reasoning,[56] to the point of view of the universe [i.e. Christ's golden rule] provides as much 'objectivity' as there can be ... This may not be enough to yield an objectively true ethical position. But it is as close to an objective basis for ethics as there is to find.[57]

Again he concedes:

> It would be nice to be able to reach a stronger conclusion than this about the basis for ethics ... the clash between self-interest and generalised benevolence, has been softened, but it has not been dissolved.[58]

Unfortunately, he does not explore the objective, rational evidence that an ultimate moral being exists, who has uniquely revealed his own character as the basis for our ethics. The existence of God, for instance, can be argued on the basis of the very existence of moral values. As philosopher William Lane Craig expresses it:[59]

- If God does not exist, objective moral values do not exist
- Evil exists
- Therefore objective moral values exist – namely, some things are evil
- Therefore God does exist

By creating humans in his image, God not only gives us an inherent foundation for our moral values, he also equips us with the intelligence we need to make moral and rational choices. Had Singer acknowledged the uniqueness of Christ's golden rule, seeing it as 'the point of view of the universe' just might have been a clue! Without such an understanding, Singer is left floundering when he writes about the meaning and significance of human life:

> The possibility of taking the point of view of the universe overcomes the problem of finding meaning in our lives, despite the ephemeral nature of human existence when measured against all the aeons of eternity.[60]

He concludes:

> Most important of all, you will know that you have not lived and died for nothing, because you will have become part of the great tradition of those who have responded to the amount of pain and suffering in the universe by trying to make the world a better place.[61]

As the violins fade, we might well ask, 'Is that enough to live by?'

Notes

[1] He has recently updated the subject in *In Defence of Animals: The Second Wave* (Blackwells, 2005)

[2] Peter Singer, *How Are We To Live?* (Oxford University Press, 1993)

[3] Peter Singer, *Ethics* (Oxford Readers (OUP), 1994) p. 5

[4] Peter Singer, *How Are We To Live?* (Opus (OUP), 1993) p. 9

[5] Singer, *How Are We To Live?* p. 5

[6] Singer stands in the tradition of the utilitarianism of Jeremy Bentham (1748-1832) and John Stuart Mill (1806-73). For more information, see New Dictionary of Christian Ethics and Pastoral Theology under 'Bentham' and 'Mill', or www.wikipedia.org/wiki/Jeremy_Bentham and www.wikipedia.org/wiki/John_Stuart_Mill

[7] Singer, *How Are We To Live?* p. 206

[8] Singer, *How Are We To Live?* p. 18

[9] Peter Singer, *Rethinking Life and Death* (Melbourne 1994) pp. 190–198

[10] Singer says that people write to him with their questions – 'whether I think prawns can feel pain,' for example (Singer, *How Are We To Live?* p. 191)

[11] Singer, *How Are We To Live?* p. 102

[12] Peter Singer, *Animal Liberation* 2nd ed. (Jonathan Cape, 1990) p. 243

[13] He allows that the Inuit, for example, may be able to justify eating animals, as they have no other option *(Practical Ethics* (CUP 1993) p. 59ff)

[14] Singer, *Practical Ethics,* p. 59ff

[15] Singer, *How Are We To Live?* pp. 18–19

[16] Singer, *How Are We To Live?* pp. 18–19.

[17] Peter Singer, 'Heavy Petting', *nerve.com*, 2001 – www.utilitarian.net/singer/by/2001----.htm

[18] Peter Singer, *Christians, Riches and Camels (Free Inquiry,* Summer 2002)

[19] Singer, *Ethics,* p. 6

[20] Singer, *How Are We To Live?* pp. 212–213

[21] Singer, *How Are We To Live?* p. 20f

[22] For instance, there are laws for the well-being of animals (e.g. Deut. 25:4). The wisdom literature teaches that, 'A righteous man cares for the needs of his animal' (Prov. 12:10). Singer also fails to notice God's compassion expressed in the story of Jonah: 'Nineveh has more than 120,000 people living in spiritual darkness, not to mention all the animals. Shouldn't I feel sorry for such a great city?' (Jon. 4:11).

[23] Mt. 6:26

[24] Mt. 8:28–34

[25] Lk. 14:5

[26] Graham Cole in Gordon Preece (ed), *Rethinking Peter Singer* (IVP 2002) p. 102

[27] See, for example, Rom. 8:19–25; Col. 1:15–23

[28] e.g. *New Dictionary of Christian Ethics and Pastoral Theology* (IVP 1995) under *Consequentialism*

[29] J. P. Moreland and William Lane Craig, *Philosophical Foundations For A Christian Woldview* (IVP, 2003) p. 438

[30] Singer, *How Are We To Live?* p. 18–19.

[31] E. Crooks and S. Briscoe, 'How to be Happy', *Financial Times,* 27 December 2003, as reported by Dean Giustini, *BMJ,* 24 December 2005

[32] Apparently, when Singer's mother was suffering from advanced Alzheimer's Disease, he paid for her nursing care himself but did not resort to euthanasia. He defended this by saying that his sister's preferences had been an important factor. See Stuart Jeffries, 'Moral Maze', *The Observer,* 23 July 2005 – books.guardian.co.uk/review/story/0,12084,1533705,00.html

[33] Gordon Preece, *Rethinking Peter Singer,* p. 26

[34] Rom. 1:18–32

[35] Singer, *Heavy Petting*

[36] The use of prostitutes in UK has apparently doubled in the past 10 years, especially among young men who buy sex much as they would any other leisure activity. (Survey reported *in Journal of Sexually Transmitted Diseases,* December 2005)

[37] Preece, *Rethinking Peter Singer*, p. 25

[38] Gal. 6:2

[39] 1 Tim. 5:8

[40] Jas. 1:27

[41] Heb. 13:2

[42] Gal. 6:9–10

[43] Singer, *How Are We To Live?* p. 19

[44] 1 Jn. 3:17–18

[45] Gal. 6:9–10, ESV

[46] Mt. 6:20

[47] Peter Singer, *Christians, Riches and Camels*

[48] Recent evidence has shown that Christians are not as mean as Singer implies. A survey of 1,200 evangelical Christians shows that they give away nine times as much as the average householder in the UK, donating, on average, 12 per cent of their net income annually (reported by Ruth Gledhill, *The Times*, 4 January 2006)

[49] Lev. 19:18; Lk. 10:25–28

[50] Lk. 10:30–35, NKJV

[51] Mt. 7:12

[52] Singer, *How Are We To Live?* p. 272

[53] Actually he names only those three of the major traditions: he cannot, for instance, find this teaching in the Koran.

[54] Mt. 6:34, NCV

[55] Singer, *How Are We To Live?* p. 275

[56] Singer wrongly asserts that others got there by reasoning. Jesus taught what the Father gave him to say (Jn. 12:49), and Christians, too, understand it by revelation through the Spirit-inspired gospel accounts of Jesus's life and teaching.

[57] Singer, *How Are We To Live?* p. 275

[58] Singer, *How Are We To Live?* p. 277

[59] William Lane Craig, *God?* (OUP, 2004) p. 126

[60] Singer, *How Are We To Live?* p. 274

[61] Singer, *How Are We To Live?* p. 280

Background to the Featured Quotes

I'd much rather be happy ... (p. xvii)

I'd much rather be happy than right any day.
Slartibartfast in the film *The Hitchhiker's Guide
to the Galaxy*

Source

The Hitchhiker's Guide to the Galaxy (dir. Garth Jennings,
Touchstone Pictures, 2005) certificate 12

Background

The Hitchhiker's Guide to the Galaxy began its highly
flexible life as a four-part radio series written by
Douglas Adams and broadcast by Radio 4. The radio
series spawned additional episodes, and was turned
into first one novel, then a 'trilogy' of five. It has also
appeared as audio recordings (which are not the same
as the radio broadcasts), a television show, a computer

game, a comic book series and finally – some twenty-five years after Adams' first discussions with Hollywood – a movie.

Adams died suddenly in 2001 at the age of forty-nine, but had already worked extensively on the script for the movie version of *The Hitchhiker's Guide to the Galaxy*. Although some fans have complained about the insertion of new material, all of the additions were written by Adams himself, who was always insistent that each new reworking of the material could not simply follow in the footsteps of previous versions of the story.

The Hitchhiker's Guide to the Galaxy tells the story of Arthur Dent (Martin Freeman) who is rescued from Earth just before it is destroyed to make way for an intergalactic by-pass. Slartibartfast (Bill Nighy) is a planet designer, who worked on the original Earth (he designed Norway and got an award for his fjords), which was in fact a supercomputer designed to determine the answer to the ultimate question of life, the universe and everything. A previous computer, Deep Thought, had been built to find the ultimate answer, which turned out to be 'forty-two'.

Sometimes we forget ... (p. 15)

Sometimes we forget the rules are there for a reason.
JD in *Scrubs*

Source

Scrubs, series three, episode ten, 'My Rule of Thumb' (NBC, 2004)

Background

Scrubs is a popular American television series set in the Sacred Heart hospital. It revolves around medical resident JD (Zack Braff), whose voiceover narrates each episode, his best friend Turk (Donald Fasion), Turk's nurse girlfriend Carla (Judy Reyes) and JD's ex-girlfriend Elliot (Sarah Chalke). The hospital is peopled with slightly psychotic patients and staff including the completely callous Dr Kelso, his nemesis, the bitter idealist Dr Cox (John C. McGinley), and the janitor (Neil Flynn) whose mission in life is to harass JD and devise new ways of annoying him.

This quote comes from one of JD's voiceovers after Turk has refused to let one of Dr Cox's patients have surgery because he drank alcohol a month before coming in (which is forbidden). Dr Cox is desperate for his patient to have surgery as he has been on the waiting list for three years, but Turk knows it is forbidden and could have disastrous results.

Some believe people are judged . . . (p. 37)

Some believe people are judged by the way they live life, and others by the way they leave it.
                                    Mary Alice in *Desperate Housewives*

Source

Desperate Housewives, episode 17, 'There Won't Be Trumpets' (ABC, 2004)

Background

Desperate Housewives is a US comedy/drama television series (broadcast on Channel 4 in the UK). Hailed as 'the new *Sex and the City*' it has been a huge success on both sides of the Atlantic. The first episode, shown in the UK on 5 January 2005, had five million viewers, beating the rating figures for the premiere of both *Friends* and *Sex and the City*.

The series centres on a group of women who live in Wisteria Lane, in American suburbia. The narrator is Mary Alice (Brenda Strong), who at the beginning of the first episode talks viewers through her own suicide. The series is an ironic look at the American ideal of the suburban family with a stay-at-home mother keeping the family together.

The quote is taken from the narrator's voice-over during episode 17 (first broadcast in the UK on 27 April 2005). The scene is the funeral of Juanita Solis, Gabrielle's mother-in-law. Carlos (Gabrielle's husband) has spent a lot of money giving his mother the best possible send-off, despite the financial difficulties he and Gabrielle are facing.

I gave them the wrong warning . . .
(p. 55)

I gave them the wrong warning. I should have told them to run as fast as they can, run and hide because the monsters are coming – the human race.

The Doctor in *Doctor Who: The Christmas Invasion*

Source

Doctor Who: The Christmas Invasion, (BBC, 2005)

Background

Doctor Who was first broadcast by BBC television in 1963, and remained a staple of the BBC schedules until 1989 – making it the longest running sci-fi television show in the world. To the delight of the show's committed fan base, it was revamped and returned for a new series in 2005. This quote comes from the Christmas special episode which was first broadcast on 25 December 2005.

The Doctor is a Time Lord from the planet Gallifrey. He travels in space and time, opposing evil and generally saving the day. He is over nine hundred years old and has two hearts. From time to time, when his body gets worn out (or when an actor gets fed up of playing the role) the Doctor regenerates. David Tennant – the Doctor quoted here – is the tenth official Doctor, following in the footsteps of William Hartnell, Patrick Troughton, Jon Pertwee, Tom Baker, Peter Davison, Colin Baker, Sylvester McCoy, Paul McGann (who played the Doctor in a single TV-movie made for the American market) and Christopher Eccleston. At the end of the 2005 series, the Doctor regenerated again, and is now played by David Tennant.

This quote comes as the Doctor has dealt with the threat of aliens invading the Earth. The Sycorax space ship is retreating, but British Prime Minister Harriet Jones (Penelope Wilton) has given orders to fire a powerful laser weapon which destroys the alien spaceship. This quote is part of the Doctor's furious response to Harriet's actions.

I think not only should you break the law ... (p. 73)

I think not only should you break the law everyday, you should be proud of it.

Benjamin Zephaniah

Source

Simon Jones, 'Dread Right?', *Third Way* magazine, Summer 2005, p. 19

Background

Benjamin Zephaniah is a poet and novelist, who has also written and presented a number of TV and radio programmes for BBC Radio Four, BBC television, ITV and Channel 4. The style of his work reflects his Jamaican heritage, and there has always been a strong theme of social justice and racial awareness in his work. He was nominated for the post of Oxford Professor of Poetry in 1989, and was considered when the post of Poet Laureate became vacant in 1999. In 2003 he turned down an OBE.

Some doctors have the Messiah complex ... (p. 89)

Some doctors have the Messiah complex; they need to save the world.

Dr Wilson in *House*

Source

House, series one, episode nine, 'DNR' (Fox, 2005)

Background

House is an American television series about Dr Gregory House (Hugh Laurie), an arrogant and anti-social doctor with a permanently bad leg which causes a limp. It follows Dr House and his team of doctors who investigate cases of puzzling medical conditions. The series received five Emmy Nominations in 2005.

This quote comes from a scene in a courtroom where Dr House is being prosecuted for saving the life of a patient who wanted to die. The patient, legendary jazz musician John Henry Giles, had signed a 'Do Not Resuscitate' (DNR) order because he had been told he was dying of a degenerative brain disorder (Amyotrophic Lateral Sclerosis). House was aware of this, but disagreed with the diagnosis and intervened to save the patient's life.

Dr House's friend, Dr Wilson (Robert Sean Leonard) has come along to the court to support him, and sits behind him so he can talk to him during the case. He goes on to say that House has a 'Rubik's complex' – he likes to solve the puzzle.

You can't make choices ... (p. 107)

You can't make choices on what you think other people's expectations will be.

Steve Carell

Source

Interview in *Total Film*, October 2005

Background

Steve Carell is an American comic actor who became known for his work on *The Daily Show* and has had supporting roles in films such as *Bruce Almighty* and *Anchorman: the Legend of Ron Burgandy*. He played David Brent in the American version of popular British TV series *The Office* and had his first lead film role in *The 40 Year Old Virgin*.

This quote comes from an interview in *Total Film* magazine when Carell is discussing how nervous he was about taking on Ricky Gervais' leading role in *The Office*.

We are the products of evolution ... (p. 117)

We are the products of evolution, not of some grand design which says this is what we are and that's it ... People say we are playing God. My answer is: 'If we don't play God, who will?'

James Watson

Source

Quoted in Sian Griffiths, *Predictions: Thirty Great Minds on the Future* (Oxford, 2000) p. 294

Background

James Watson is best known for his discovery, with Francis Crick, of the structure of DNA in 1953 while he was working at the Cavendish Laboratory in the University of Cambridge. He and Crick were awarded the Nobel Prize for Physiology or Medicine in 1962 (along with Maurice Wilkins, whose work they incorporated).

In 1988, Watson was appointed Head of the Human Genome Project (part of the America National Institutes of Health (NIH)), a position he held until 1992. He resigned after a conflict with the head of the NIH Bernardine Healy. Watson believed Healy was wrong to try to commercialise genes by granting patents on them. Like Crick, Watson is a convinced atheist and has a reputation for being outspoken on issues of religion and politics as well as science.

It's not who you are underneath … (p. 129)

It's not who you are underneath. It's what you do that defines you.

Rachel Dawes in the film *Batman Begins*

Source

Batman Begins (dir. Christopher Nolan, Warner Brothers, 2005) certificate 12

Background

Batman Begins is the first new Batman film since 1997's poorly received *Batman and Robin*. British director Christopher Nolan, who made his name with *Memento*, has taken the reins of the franchise, and offers a darker portrayal of the central character which owes much to the influence of Frank Miller's *Dark Knight* comic strip.

Rachel Dawes (Katie Holmes) is a childhood friend of Bruce Wayne (Christian Bale). While he secretly becomes Batman, she becomes a prosecutor at the District Attorney's office, and is idealistically committed to opposing the culture of corruption that allows criminals to rule Gotham City.

This quote first occurs when Rachel is berating Bruce for his indulgent playboy lifestyle, unaware that this is merely a front for his caped-crusading alter ego. Later in the film, after Batman has saved Rachel's life and she asks him who he is, he replies by echoing these words – Rachel's first hint that Bruce is not the disappointment that she thought him to be.

For Further Reading

Charles Colson and Nigel M. de S. Cameron (eds.), *Human Dignity and the Biotech Century* (IVP (USA), 2004)

Francis Fukuyama, *Our Posthuman Future: Consequences of the Biotechnology Revolution* (Profile Books, 2002)

Philip Hefner, *Technology and Human Becoming* (Fortress Press, 2003)

John Frederic Kilner, C. Christopher Hook and Diane B. Uustal (eds.), *Cutting Edge Bioethics* (Eerdmans, 2002)

Gilbert Meilaender, *Bioethics: a Primer for Christians* (Paternoster, 1999)

Peter Moore, *Babel's Shadow: Genetic Technologies in a Fracturing Society* (Lion, 2000)

Gordon Preece (ed), *Rethinking Peter Singer* (IVP, 2002)

Gregory Stock, *Redesigning Humans* (Profile Books, 2002)

John Wyatt, *Matters of Life and Death* (IVP, 1998)

Other titles in the *Talking About* Series

Sex and the Cynics: Talking About the Search for Love

Truth Wars: Talking About Tolerance

Spooked: Talking About the Supernatural

Other titles from Damaris Books

Get More Like Jesus While Watching TV
by Nick Pollard and Steve Couch

Teenagers: Why Do They Do That?
by Nick Pollard

Saving Sex: Answers to Teenagers' Questions About Relationships and Sex (due for publication Spring 2006)
by Dr Trevor Stammers and Tim Doak

Back In Time: A thinking fan's guide to Doctor Who
by Steve Couch, Tony Watkins and Peter S. Williams

Dark Matter: A thinking fan's guide to Philip Pullman
by Tony Watkins

Matrix Revelations: A thinking fan's guide to the Matrix trilogy
edited by Steve Couch

I Wish I Could Believe In Meaning
by Peter S. Williams

If Only
by Nick Pollard

Join Damaris and receive

Discounts on other products from Damaris Books and Damaris Publishing.

Access to Web pages containing up-to-date information about popular culture.

To find out about **free membership** of Damaris go to www.damaris.org

www.damaris.org

CultureWatch
(free access website)

CultureWatch explores the message behind the media through hundreds of articles and study guides on films, books, music and television. It is written from a distinctively Christian angle, but is appropriate for people of all faiths and people of no faith at all.

CULTUREWATCH
http://www.damaris.org/cw

The Quest
(CD ROM)

Your journey into the heart of spirituality.

Take your own route, take your own time, seek your own answers to the big philosophical and religious questions with this self-updating oracle for your PC.

The Quest grows as you search, with free updates automatically downloaded from the Web.

THE **Q**UEST

www.questforanswers.com